Billy Steel

Scotland's Little Maestro

Billy Steel

Scotland's Little Maestro

Bob MacAlindin

TEMPUS

First published 2003

Tempus Publishing Limited
The Mill, Brimscombe Port,
Stroud, Gloucestershire, GL5 2QG

British Library Cataloguing in Publication Data.
A catalogue record for this book is available from the British Library.

ISBN 0 7524 2874 8

Typesetting and origination by Tempus Publishing Limited
Printed in Great Britain by Midway Colour Print, Wiltshire

Contents

Acknowledgements

The author wishes to make clear his appreciation of the assistance rendered by Chris Wraight in the selection and presentation of photographs for this publication, by John Lister for allowing access to his substantial football records and to Neil Cosgrove, Dave Forbes, Lawrie Reilly, Bobby Cox, Lorraine Watt, Charles Wellwood, Graham Hughes and Jim Dick.

Introduction

When Scotland failed to qualify for the final stages of football's World Cup during the summer of 2001, I breathed a sigh of relief. Odd, you might think, for a Scot, and a lifelong fan of football. Yet there's an inescapable logic behind the reason for that sigh. Try as I might, I could detect no route through the maze of mediocrity in which our present national side seems doomed to wander to visualise how we might have begun to cope with the likes of Brazil, Spain and, yes, even England. It is not the fault of the players that no individual in that squad merits the label world-class, a term by the way, ludicrously applied by some commentators to a few of our footballers of the relatively recent past. Such verbal incontinence finds its origins in an almost total lack of awareness of what's going on elsewhere in the world. Thus it can happen that amid a general feeling of astonishment an ageing 'unknown' like Lubomir Moravcik arrives from the shadows of central Europe to assume without difficulty the mantle of the most technically gifted footballer in the country. Moravcik has come and gone but he leaves behind him, like a signature in an autograph book, an indelible reminder of exactly how far behind we have fallen.

Over the last twenty years I can think of no Scot who would merit inclusion in any World XI with the possible but unlikely exception of Dalglish. He was a superb player, no doubt about it, but one who could dwell fractionally too long on the ball. I witnessed a classic example of this in the all-seater stadium at Frankfurt when Scotland, playing in white, drew 1-1 with Yugoslavia in the 1974 World Cup finals. Midway through the first half, Dalglish found himself with half a second or so in which to strike for goal. The situation cried out for a first-time shot, but he took a touch and both ball and opportunity promptly disappeared.

To find the reason why we are condemned to dwell in our present-day footballing desert, one need only look at the state of the game in our part of the world.

Football in Scotland – I refuse to call it Scottish football – has for years been riddled with foreign players, a few of whom are class acts, while the others among them have landed lucrative berths here for the excellent reason that nobody else would have them. These mercenaries feast on the corpse of a long-dead footballing giant, formerly of world-wide renown as a nursery for players of real poise and flair. Perhaps *the* most depressing aspect is this – for all the pedestrian nature of this particular group of 'stars' they still possess more craft than the home-grown product, which despite a glimmer of hope to be found in some of the young players now starting to make their mark, remains as I write, about 95 per cent endeavour and 5 per cent guile.

While acknowledging the existence of the aforesaid glimmer, I do not share the hopelessly optimistic assessments of this crop of new young players. One or two might rise above the ordinary, but what we have in the main is nothing more than a future bunch of yet more honest toilers. Therefore, unrestrained as I am by any requirement to express myself in diplomatic terms, I have no hesitation in labelling the standard of our domestic football as rock bottom.

The comparison between skill levels of today and of my own earliest era as a spectator, the late 1940s and early 1950s, I find I can for the sake of convenience crystallize into a single element – the routine cross ball into the penalty area.

It never fails to amaze me how seldom the standard of such a ball reaches acceptable levels in the modern era, the latest World Cup providing many an example. In my time wingers like Ally Gunn of Dundee and Aberdeen's Jackie Hather – by no means players of international calibre – seemed able to put in wonderful crosses time after time, the ball bending away from the 'keeper and into that zone where on-rushing forwards would wish to find it. They even had a different name for the exercise – centring the ball – and that's what they did as if in their sleep, they centred it. One day the penny must drop on why Beckham is such an important player for his club and for England – he can actually do this relatively simple thing.

The greatest wingman produced by British football in the twentieth century is by common consent Stanley Matthews of Stoke City, Blackpool and England. The man was a perfectionist to the point where if he did not have a specific player to aim at with his centre, he set himself to placing every cross ball precisely eight yards out from the goal line.

I hope it may be seen then, that from such a puerile present it is natural enough to look back on what used to be. Those football memories I am about to recall are from a time the world has all but forgotten, existing nowadays only in the minds of old fogeys like me. And through my own retrospective salute to one particular player, which is the true object of this exercise, I hope to be able to illustrate the gulf in overall class between then and now.

My hero is the best player I ever saw 'live' and I've watched Law, Baxter, Jimmy Johnstone, Dalglish, that gifted Irishman Peter Doherty, Yugoslav midfield maestro Branton Oblak and Zoltan Varga. Who? Exactly. The point I have just made, using Moravcik as the example, could apply to Varga only more so. While staying in Aberdeen in the early 1970s I was a regular at Pittodrie to watch the Dons, who had acquired the Hungarian Varga for a spell. Nobody had heard of him, yet the man was possessed of a poise so natural that everything going on around him leaked an air of frantic incompetence. He could direct 40-yard passes with stunning accuracy, drift past players as though they did not exist and stood out a mile in the Scottish game.

He was a huge hit at Aberdeen and I recall standing on the terracing when a nearby fan, struggling to articulate the ultimate view on yet another wonderful pass, found it in the phrase: 'Aw, whit a ba' Zoaltun!' It did not seem to matter that the person at whom the comment was directed could not have heard it and that had he heard it, there was no way he could have understood. Although a different type of player, Varga reminded me in some respects of my own great favourite, who was one of such a number at the time he was at his peak that Scotland could have delivered onto the pitch two elevens, each capable of taking on the best the world had to offer.

In retrospect that's hardly surprising. Virtually every man in Scotland's senior game was a Scot, with a sprinkling of homegrown stardust also helping to enhance the scene south of the Border.

And of course, those were the ones who had made it to the senior grade. They were the best of a truly enormous bunch. Everybody played. On the streets and in back alleys the sound of a rubber ball or an old tennis ball rebounding from a wall was something you woke up to every weekend and it continued virtually without pause until it grew dark. In the after-school hours the lure of the game meant you often missed your tea. Lads learned how to kill a spiteful rebound on thighs, insteps and tummies, acquiring without realising it a degree of ball control that would have modern coaches salivating with envy. It was the era of the 'tanner ba' player, an expression carrying with it an implied scorn but actually was a highly accurate way of describing how top exponents of the game came by the skills so conspicuous by their absence today.

Football pitches were swamped with fixtures, one succeeding another as Saturdays passed by in a welter of activity. I can recall the 30 pitches at Riverside Park, Dundee all in use at the same time – 30 referees, 60 linesmen and 660 players. It is impossible to contemplate such a thing today with teenage zombies living out their waking-dead moments transfixed in front of television monitors pressing buttons as in some hideous pre-programmed existence which, in a sense, it is. This is nothing like the whole story of course. Boys in most other lands play computer games too. Take France as an example. Despite their disappointing show in the World Cup, they are reaping the rewards of a comprehensive and heavily-funded football education and coaching system set up in the 1980s by, among others, the Liverpool manager Gérard Houllier.

In the late 1940s and early 1950s, Scottish football however, was self-taught and on the back of an instinctive eagerness to learn, it worked well enough. All that has gone and like boxing during the Depression years of the 1930s, when an undisputed world champion at any weight was at the top of a massive pile of pugilists, football gives the lie to the modern myth that sporting skills must always improve with the passage of time. What *has* improved is the standard of training and fitness, especially with most players today being full-time professionals, but these aspects inhabit the mere margins of the game which ought to be, above all else, a showpiece for skill in the use of the ball.

Boys like myself, steeped in football and completely spoiled for choice, speculated endlessly upon which was the best team Scotland could put out. A much-touted combination was the Rangers 'Iron Curtain' defence and the entire Hibernian forward line – the Famous Five – Smith, Johnstone, Reilly, Turnbull and Ormond, who in Scotland at least really pioneered the art of interchanging with one another, always setting different problems for defences. The Rangers/Hibs selection never happened of course but oh, what a team that would have been!

Come the end of the Second World War, football returned from being of necessity a part-time pastime to its normal top billing in the sporting make-up of a nation dog-tired and broke after six years of conflict. We needed perking up and on the parks of the major clubs in Scotland we got it – in spades. The Scottish League (Division 'A'), yesterday's equivalent of the Scottish Premier League, was no two-horse race.

As well as Rangers and Celtic, teams such as Aberdeen, Third Lanark, St Johnstone, Dundee, Hearts, Hibs, Raith Rovers, Motherwell, East Fife, Clyde and Partick Thistle all had players on their books to offer a serious challenge for honours.

In international terms, between 1946 and 1954, which is the principal period here, Scotland showed herself able to compete on more or less level terms with England, who had a vastly greater number of players to choose from. The English in those days bestrode the world of football like a Colossus.

For me, from a host of skilled exponents who ran out of the gloom of the players' tunnel into the pure winter light, one stood out. Through an almost magical spring in his own step he put an added spring into mine. His name was Billy Steel.

As a youngster who followed the game with fanatical zeal and who completed several scrapbooks of newspaper pictures and cuttings from the period, I gained an early awareness of his existence. I first heard of him during the war as he exhibited his talents with Greenock Morton, but the story had begun long before that.

-1-
Early Days

Billy was born on 1 May 1923 in Denny, Stirlingshire, in the same street as Jimmy McMullan, who played for Partick Thistle and Manchester City and who in 1928 captained the Wembley Wizards, the team which sent England crashing to a 5–1 defeat.

It is surely appropriate that Billy first saw the light of day in an age when Scottish football was the envy of the world. Although the sport was an English invention, it was the Scots who altered it from an exercise in individual skills like dribbling and shooting to a genuine team effort. They set the precedent – and the standard – for passing the ball, which was kept almost exclusively on the ground. A remarkable example of this features one of the star forwards of the period, Alan Morton of Rangers (the Wee Blue Devil). In the entire span of his international career, Morton never once scored with his head.

As a toddler, Billy was given a pair of football boots one Christmas by his grandfather to stop him kicking the toes out of his shoes. Football was in his blood. Billy's first serious brush with the game occurred on a scorching June day as he settled down to watch a practice session for a five-a-side competition which was to be one of the star attractions of the gala day in his home town. 'Wee Wullie' as he was dubbed on account of his tiny frame, was invited to join one team which was a man short and he did so well on the big day for this 'no hoper' outfit that they reached the final. It proved to be the initial step towards realising his destiny, which was to become the Golden Boy of Football.

During his last year of formal education, 'Wee Wullie's' school team won every competition they entered by which time their star player had already turned out three times for the Scottish Schoolboys. The first of these appearances was against Wales in 1937 at the Vetch Field, Swansea when the Scots lost 2-1. The boys were shaken by a terrible injury to their outside right whose broken leg bone was sticking right out through his football sock. Only at a theatre that evening did the youngsters begin to get over that trauma as they listened to no less a performer than Max Miller crack several jokes at their expense.

In the second international, against England at Cowdenbeath, Fife, Scotland again lost their outside right, Bobby Wilson, who broke his wrist! The visitors won 4-3, Billy having played for the first time alongside George Young, with whom he would star on many future occasions in the full international side. That day Billy was in direct opposition to a lad by the name of Foulkes, who would go on to play professional football for Walsall. In one clash as they both went for the ball, Foulkes, a full head taller than Billy, was knocked unconscious and had to be carried off. After the match Billy asked him how he felt and was told: 'It wasn't the injury that bothered me. But to be knocked out by someone your size was just too bad!'

Young, in his book *Captain of Scotland*, made reference to his games with Billy in these schoolboy internationals.

He wrote: 'Our inside left, a tiny fellow who could make a football do everything but name its maker, was an outstanding success. With his Eddie Cantor-like eyes, elfish sense of humour and personality, this little fellow with the big heart became my friend. As we used to walk along together, he in his shorts, me in my long trousers, we were often referred to as "Mutt and Jeff".'

Billy's final schoolboy's cap was awarded, still in 1937, as Scotland dismantled Ireland at Grosvenor Park, Belfast. Steel, this time in the inside-right position, scored a hat-trick before half-time. During his interval pep talk, the Scotland trainer turned to Billy and said: 'You needn't think you're playing a good game just because you've scored three goals!'

In the summer of that year Billy, now aged fourteen, signed for Dunipace Thistle who competed in the Stirlingshire Secondary Juvenile League. This was strictly an amateur set-up and the league carried an upper-age limit of twenty. Still a tiny figure despite having lost the 'Wee Wullie' tag, Billy often looked completely out of place beside the bigger, older lads although not as far as football ability was concerned!

An especially close rivalry existed between the Thistle and Denny and Dunipace YMCA and Billy was able to recall in later life a most satisfying match when the Thistle knocked YM out of the Scottish Secondary Juvenile Cup – on their own ground.

During 1938, as a consequence of needing some pocket money for a holiday, Billy signed as a professional for Bo'ness Cadora, a junior club. He wasn't there long. He just happened to be playing 'a blinder' against Lochgelly Violet in a Scottish Junior Cup tie when the brother of Leicester City manager Johnnie Duncan was in the crowd. Succumbing to some gentle persuasion from scout Walter McLean, with whom Billy would form a lifelong friendship, the lad agreed to join the Leicester City groundstaff. His football in the Midlands was played in the Colts side and he formed a great left-wing partnership with Charlie Adam, who eventually graduated to the first team. It was one of very few plusses for Billy however, who became homesick and returned to Scotland within a year.

With some difficulty he got himself re-instated as an amateur and signed as such for St Mirren for the 1939/40 season. After he had starred in a practice match he was flabbergasted, on his sixteenth birthday, to find himself selected for St Mirren's First XI to take on the mighty Glasgow Rangers. It turned out to be a disheartening experience. 'I hardly saw the ball all afternoon,' Billy recalled.

The match seemed to affect him badly for he lost his form and for weeks could hardly put a foot right. He was farmed out to an amateur club before battling his way back into the St Mirren team in time to give a stunning exhibition against Greenock Morton, who, remembering what had been for them a painful encounter, signed Billy as a professional on his seventeenth birthday. This trans- action was carried through on the very first day the club were per- mitted to do it, and Billy left the ground with £50 burning a hole in his back pocket. It was a turning point. He was happy at the club and was greatly helped by trainer Jimmy Gourlay who taught him to put his setbacks behind him and concentrate on the task in hand.

Billy also never forgot his first match in a Morton jersey. Left half Jimmy Whyte, known as 'the iron man', took him aside before the game and said: 'Don't worry about a thing, son. I'll be right behind you all the time.'

At Greenock, Billy struck up a fine partnership with the tall, rangy inside right, Tommy Orr, and both gained immensely from the experience of centre forward Johnny Crum, who had once worn the blue shirt of Scotland.

It was with Morton that Billy found the fighting spirit that was to characterise his career and it was also where he got to see some of football's greats up close, the English stars Tommy Lawton and Stanley Matthews sometimes guesting for the club during the war years.

Morton's 1941/42 season was one of the best in the club's history. They were runners-up to Rangers in the League and were unlucky to lose to the Glasgow side in the final of the League Cup. This match was to prove a memorable one for Billy − for all the wrong reasons. He struggled through the 90 minutes enshrouded in a mist of pain, still able to produce some of the brilliant thrusts that were already a Steel trademark.

At the end of the match he staggered off, clearly in trouble and had to be rushed to hospital where he underwent an emergency appendix operation. He should never have played and he was extremely lucky even to get permission to play. He had joined the Army just five days before and it was only with great difficulty that he had got the nod from his commanding officer to take part in the game. During the following two years, Billy continued to represent Morton, the needs of the Royal Corps of Signals having priority however. In his unit, he was lucky to have as mates several gifted footballers, including Tommy Walker (Hearts), Bobby Campbell (Falkirk), George Sutherland (Partick Thistle) and Jimmy Carabine, who would go on to manage Third Lanark.

In 1944 Steel's unit landed in France and went on to 'visit' Holland and Germany. 'Just a few games of football with the section', was how Billy described his Army life on the Continent. It was a massive understatement.

At the beginning of 1945 the section was resting at Amiens, France. A fixture was arranged with the locals who, before the match began, bowed solemnly to all parts of the field, to the astonishment of the British players and the watching soldiers.

The war tugged the section into Germany, and, on a pitch near Hamburg, Billy and his mates played a team consisting entirely of displaced Italians.

The pitch was mostly sand and every time the ball was kicked anyone close was almost blinded. In another match Billy received a crack on the ankle which was not properly diagnosed and he ended up in hospital in Hanover for quite a spell where it received proper treatment.

Fit again, he rejoined the unit, whose commanding officer was football mad. The unit team trained as if they were a League side and they went on to take the championship for the units in their district, winning one game 17-0, in the process of which Steel scored nine goals! The quartermaster had promised the players an extra two cigarettes apiece in their ration packs if they scored 22 goals. For their 'near miss' they got them anyway!

Billy always referred to this time in Germany as one of the happiest of his life. He was playing so well that his CO recommended him for the BAOR team (British Army on the Rhine) who at that stage had a staff of 39 players, including 22 internationals. Among those Billy played with were Leslie Compton, Eddie Hapgood and Matt Busby.

Billy considered Matt one of the best wing-halves he ever saw. He said: 'I had the pleasure of playing with him in several Army teams. To play inside forward in front of him was a real joy; all that was required was for me to run into an open space and there was the ball, more often than not placed perfectly at my feet. I have seen Matt beat three men with one brilliant pass.'

Billy highlighted another of Matt's strengths – his quick thinking. Writing about the advantages of 'selling the dummy', he recalled one match at Dumfries in wartime when Matt was playing for a Scottish select against Steel's Army side which on that occasion included Lawton, Cliff Britton, Joe Mercer, goalkeeper Frank Swift, Jimmy Carabine and Jimmy Hagan of Sheffield United and England.

'The incident, one I most vividly remember, occurred during a corner. Johnny Deakin of St Mirren took the kick and placed it further away from Frank Swift than usual. Matt was standing there about 20 yards from goal. He prepared to head the ball into the crowded goalmouth. Well, the header that beats Frank Swift must be some header from that distance. But Matt had a trick to come. At the last second he jumped a little and broke the force of the ball with his chest and as it fell to the ground he shot with great force, just missing the goal by inches. The action of preparing to head had completely deceived everyone. If the defence had had the slightest idea he was going to shoot, they would have rushed out and blocked his shot.'

Billy's games for BAOR included two in the Channel Islands, at St Helier (Jersey) and on Guernsey. The opposition didn't amount to much, the St Helier game ending 10-2, but with the wonderful welcome received by the players, no one cared!

The Army administrators did manage to strike one sour note. In accommodating the players they had selected one hotel for the 'other ranks' and a higher quality one for the officers in the team.

The officers wouldn't have it and the entire group settled into the lesser hotel, fully expecting some official backlash. The Army did seem to have learned from the experience, however, and the players got away with what was a flagrant breach of orders.

Back in Germany, the team was dispersed to their various units until March 1946 when they were reunited to tackle some teams from Britain. The first match, against Portsmouth at Hanover, ended with BAOR winning 3-1 but only after a huge squad of helpers had removed a covering of snow from the ground. After the match, all the players enjoyed the luxury of an ice-cold shower, there being not a drop of hot water in the place!

Billy's side then beat Manchester United 2-1, even though several Army stars were not available for the match. In the next game, at Munster, Everton proved too strong for the Army, who suffered their first defeat, thanks to a majestic performance from Wally Boyes.

They were back to their winning ways at Antwerp as BAOR took on a team representing the Central Mediterranean Forces, who were able to field players of the calibre of Willie Thornton (Rangers), Tom Finney (Preston North End), Jimmy Rudd (Manchester City), George Wilkins (Brentford) and Steel's old pal Charlie Adam (Leicester City).

The BAOR boys then undertook a brief tour of Poland. None had any passports and they were almost turned back at the airfield in Warsaw. However, the crisis was resolved, thanks to the direct intervention of the country's President, and the Poles went on to win the first game at Krakow, Silesia, 3-2. This was perhaps not too surprising, since, finding themselves 2-1 down at half-time, they introduced seven substitutes!

But if the Britons thought that game a bit strange, it was nothing compared to the next, at Katowice, which ended in a draw. In the first 10 minutes there was more deliberate kicking than was seen in a full season in Britain. The match crawled with tension, not helped by the field being surrounded by a towering wire fence. This did not deter the spectators, who quickly found their range over the fence and began to pelt the visitors with stones.

In an attempt to keep this barrage of boulders within reasonable bounds, Polish soldiers were brought in, stationed every few yards around the pitch. The British players would remember for the rest of their days the murderous looks they got from the crowd.

Back in Krakow, Polish officials produced a major miracle in the midst of chronic food shortages and laid on a breakfast for their visitors comprising of three eggs, a piece of bacon measuring six inches square for each player, masses of butter and fresh rolls, and that same evening provided such a banquet that it took the British party three hours to dispose of it.

Next on the team's itinerary – Switzerland. The town of Basle was the first stop and although just an hour away from the border with Germany what a change from that devastated country! Billy and his team-mates found themselves in the lap of luxury in a land which had managed to remain neutral for the entire six years of war.

The first match, at Lausanne, featured the national team and the Army won 2-1. They were slightly taken aback to find themselves described in the local press as 'training partners to the Swiss national side'.

On the way to Arau, a small town which was the venue for the next game, the party came within a hair's breadth of disaster. During a stiff mountain climb, the 39-seater bus skidded on a corner and ended with one wheel just six inches away from a 200-foot drop.

The match was won with something to spare and the tourists, for that is now how they felt during this June sortie, could not believe their luck as they lay sun-bathing by a hotel pool in Interlaken with snow-capped mountains in the background. The thought of returning to the ruins of Germany did not appeal at all. At Basle they took on a local police team on a scorcher of a day and managed to win 4-0 despite merely ambling round the pitch. Each player received the gift of a magnificent wristwatch.

In Berne, a match was played under floodlights and the BAOR footballers found this an oddity, being suddenly unsure of their techniques, and they only drew the game. The players received a visit before the match from an old friend, Tommy Lawton, who seemed to be engaged in giving summer soccer courses to just about everybody.

Back in Germany, Billy played in a number of matches of varying importance before the team broke up for leave. After the visit home, the side re-formed for a tournament comprising all the nations which could field teams in the European theatre of operations. The BAOR side were due to tackle a Russian select but the men from Moscow scratched and the first match was against Denmark in Hamburg which ended in a win, as did the second game when Norway were the opponents.

The semi-final against Holland in Lyons looked like being a tough test for the Dutch were reputed to be a class outfit. Partly due to the sheer brilliance of Billy Steel however, the Britons won with ease.

A return to Berlin via Paris allowed the British team enough time for some serious training in preparation for the final in which they would face Czechoslovakia. The match, in the Olympic Stadium, was a massive celebration of the peace and of football. Nine goals were scored, six of them by Britons. Steel got his winners' medal along with the others from Sir Sholto Douglas, the then Commander-in-Chief of BAOR.

Far from Britain it may have been, but interest in the exploits of the Army footballers was high and now Billy was about to reap the reward for a number of mesmerising performances throughout Europe which earned him the nickname 'little perpetual motion.'

He was demobbed from the Army in December 1946 and resumed his career as a part-time footballer with Morton, having also taken as a day job a post at Denny town hall.

By now a world record transfer fee was being openly talked about as several English clubs were plainly interested. When Billy illuminated the whole match in his very first full international against England at Wembley on 12 April 1947, the rustle of cheque books could be heard throughout the footballing world. Little wonder.

BBC radio commentator Raymond Glendenning, in his foreword to Billy's own book, *How To Play Football*, recalled the game:

'That was the day I had my first sight of soccer's Blond Bombshell,' he wrote. 'In a dark blue jersey with a large number 10 on his back, he walked sedately across the famous Wembley turf and lined up with his colleagues on one side of the Royal Tunnel.

'After the game my thoughts kept by-passing the thrills of that hectic 90 minutes and going back to the sight of this stocky Scot, his fair hair well plastered down as he stood motionless and without the slightest trace of nerves, waiting for the preliminaries to be got over. By the way he raced off as the lines eventually broke up to indulge in a few leg-loosening strides and pre-match shots at goal, I could sense he was at the top of his form. And so it proved.'

Billy described that first match for his country as his greatest-ever footballing thrill. He was one of seven new 'caps'. Given no chance against an all-conquering England side – reckoned by many experts to be the finest ever – the Scots surprised everyone except themselves by earning a 1-1 draw. Playing immediately behind Steel in the left-half position was Dundonian Alec 'Red' Forbes who recalled the match in an article in the *Sporting Post* on 8 May 1954.

'That team was the finest I ever played with,' wrote Forbes. The line-up, playing the usual 1, 2, 3, 5 formation read: Miller (Celtic); Young (Rangers), Shaw (Rangers); Macauley (Brentford), Woodburn (Rangers), Forbes (Sheffield United); Smith (Hibs), McLaren (Preston North End), Delaney (Manchester United), Steel (Morton), Pearson (Newcastle United).

As *The Times* of 14 April had it: 'At five minutes to three Scotland were given no chance. In the end however, it was to Scotland went the glory.'

Scotland had led 1-0 at half-time through a goal by Andy McLaren and although England equalised through Horatio 'Raich' Carter, by quarter to five the home side were hanging on for the draw and only two daring saves by Frank Swift when he dived at the feet of first Delaney and then Steel, rescued his team from defeat.

The draw was all the more remarkable since the English League had outplayed the Scottish League (minus Steel) at Hampden on 12 March, winning 3-1. The tables were turned at Wembley to such an extent that it took England 33 minutes to win their first corner.

George Young considered that match a great tactical success. In order to cut off the supply of passes to Stanley Matthews, Forbes and Macauley were handed the task of getting on top of the England inside forward pair, Carter and Wilf Mannion from the outset. (Forbes came into football by pure chance. After leaving school in his native Dundee, he decided that ice hockey was the game for him. He worked very hard at learning the arts of this hugely physical sport and was soon being mentioned as a player of great promise. Then by sheer chance, Alex took a walk to a local park and met an old friend who was bemoaning the fact that the football team he was helping to manage had only 10 players. 'Could you help us out, Alex?' he pleaded. Forbes stepped into the breach and played a 'blinder'. The rest is history.) The wing-halves, Young noted, had to work overtime − 'without a thought of overtime rates' − and the Matthews threat was duly contained. They, and Steel, were the men of the match.

As was generally the case at Wembley, the Scottish supporters were also men of the match, turning the stadium into a virtual home ground contest for their country. They had reached the venue only with the greatest difficulty. A ban on railway specials to sporting events had been introduced in order to save coal and although some groups hired coaches, for the bulk of the remainder of the 29,000 Scots who had purchased tickets, the normal train services had to take the strain. This meant spreading the travel over several days to allow the railway to cope. Many Scots who arrived early as a result slept rough; some hitch-hiked; a few hired cars in an age when car hire was almost unknown; motor bikes and side cars were pressed into use. It is probably true to say that everyone with a ticket got there somehow.

Not surprisingly, the Scottish selectors chose the same team for the first post-war continental tour to play Belgium, Luxembourg and the BAOR side in Hamburg, but it was on a much bigger stage in the wake of that tour that Billy Steel was to provide the football world with another example of his burgeoning genius.

I still had never seen Billy play, but through the medium of my scrapbooks I was able to savour, second-hand as it were, his goal for the Great Britain side against the Rest of Europe at Hampden before a crowd of 134,000 on Saturday 10 May 1947.

It is staggering to think that the crowd was *limited* on police advice to 134,000, Hampden's capacity at that time being 150,000. The national stadium was by far the largest in the British Isles. The biggest-ever crowd to watch a football match in Britain saw 149,547 people click through Hampden's 130 turn-stiles to take in the Scotland-England encounter of 1937. Little wonder the famous Hampden roar could be heard fifteen miles from the ground.

In what was described as 'the match of the century' the Great Britain team won 6-1. The team: Swift (England), Hardwick (England), Hughes (Wales); Macauley (Scotland), Vernon (Northern Ireland), Burgess (Wales); Matthews (England), Mannion (England), Lawton (England), Steel (Scotland), Liddell (Scotland).

For this glittering occasion, Billy, the youngest man on the park, opted to wear a very old pair of football boots. In this dubious footwear he proceeded to dominate the match. Having laid on a goal for Wilf Mannion, Billy collected the ball in the centre circle shortly after.

Raymond Glendenning took up the story: 'It was the 34th minute. From the halfway line Steel cut his way through the conti-nental defence like a hot knife through butter.'

Billy had noticed the European defenders backing off, waiting for the pass that must surely come. It never did. Thirty yards out he let fly with a left-foot shot that almost burst the net.

What French goalkeeper Julian da Rui thought about it is not on record. Known in his home country as 'The India Rubber Man' on account of his athleticism, he was reduced by the venom of Steel's drive to a figure of statuesque impotence.

That effort, described by Matthews after the game as 'a most wonderful goal', remains to this day on the short list of the greatest goals ever scored at Hampden. Giving added weight to Steel's counter, if that is the right expression, it is worth noting that the 1940s football was heavier than the modern version. Taxing the scales at about 1lb (around 500g) and comprising an outer skin of leather and an inner tube of rubber, its propulsion at pace required greater effort than today, especially on a wet afternoon when the ball could absorb moisture. Leather for the outer skin was cut into a variety of shapes, each one stitched to the next to make up the whole. One version was the T ball, where every shape was formed to resemble a capital T. These old-style footballs also carried a lace, to close up the slit into which the rubber tube had to be inserted before inflation, usually with a bicycle pump.

Playing in his usual position of inside left, Billy formed a deadly partnership with Liddell, but although the two were within yards of one another throughout the game, even the Liverpool winger had no notion of what befell Steel just after half-time.

A stud nail in Billy's right boot broke through the worn sole and penetrated his foot. Masking the pain, Billy continued to thrill the crowd with his own unique brand of soccer wizardry. In the dressing room at full-time, his team mates could not believe what they saw when he pulled off his boot. The sock was soaked in blood almost to the ankle. The match fee? £14 per player, £6 less than the fee for a genuine international.

One extraordinary statistic emerged from the game. During the entire ninety minutes not a single deliberate foul was recorded.

Lawrie Reilly, the former Hibernian and Scotland forward, recalled in a recent interview how painful it could be to head the ball if it was not met just right. After an 'off centre' header in one match for the Scottish League side he was in a state of such concussion that he remembers nothing about it. His Hibernian colleague, Gordon Smith, likened playing with that ball to 'kicking a brick'.

The Scots' European tour, which was sandwiched between the England-Scotland match and the Britain *v.* Europe game, had got under way with an almighty scare for the players. Most of them were flying for the first time and as the team's propeller-driven Dakota aircraft came in to land at Brussels airport it overshot the runway. The pilot managed to claw his plane back into the air and to land successfully at the second time of asking. Steel never forgot the incident however, and hated flying from that moment on.

The Scots lost 2-1 to Belgium at the Stade du Heysel on Sunday 18 May, Steel scoring for the visitors in the 64th minute. It was a disappointing start to the tour but hardly surprising given the state of the pitch. For the duration of the German occupation it had been used as a tank park and some deep ruts caused by these vehicles were still in evidence.

Nevertheless, the surface was the same for both sides and the Belgians, with right-winger Victor Lemberechts and inside left Joe Mermans particularly outstanding, richly deserved their win.

During the match Billy Steel sustained an injury to his jaw and, with some gentle persuasion from George Young, he visited a dentist in Brussels. Recollecting the incident, Young wrote: 'The dentist, a keen football fan, took considerable trouble over the job and eventually wired one loose tooth to an adjoining one. Then came a shock for Billy. The dentist announced that there was nothing he could do for the other loose tooth. He produced a pair of pliers and before Steel or I realised that he was going to start work without giving any form of anaesthetic he had extracted the tooth. As I had suggested taking Billy to the dentist in the first place I felt a very guilty fellow as the wee lad turned to me – and grinned.'

Just before the start of the game against Luxembourg, one local official told George Young that the match ball was going to be dropped from a plane! Young thought it was a joke but sure enough, the drone of an approaching aircraft was soon heard. Out of the sky dived a small two-seater and with an accuracy that would have delighted any bomb aimer, the pilot let go of the ball which hit the ground almost on the centre circle. It bounced back so high that he could have caught it again but when the ball did finally come to rest, the adventure had clearly proved a deflating one and it had gone soft. With a new ball, the Scots ran out winners by 6-1.

The game against BAOR resulted in a 2-1 loss, the Scots having done some disastrous experimenting, including playing Young at centre forward!

-2-
International Glory

Back in Britain, Billy's career took a gigantic leap forward when, in June 1947, he signed for Derby County for a then world record £15,500. Oddly enough, he was not the first Billy Steel to sign for the club, since a left back of that name, also a Scot, had joined them in 1939 for £1,275. After all the circumstances of the signing of the latter Billy were known, there was much surprise expressed for it was revealed that plans had been laid by Derby years before to acquire the services of the brilliant little Scot.

Stuart McMillan, Derby's manager and one of the finest judges of a player in the game, had had his eye on Billy even before he had joined the Army. McMillan grabbed the chance of a quick word with Steel before the Scotland party went on tour and with the memory of Billy's great match at Wembley as well as his showing for the Great Britain side still fresh in the mind, the pace hotted up. When the young Scot returned from Europe he was asked to make his way to Greenock without delay. The deal was quickly struck, with McMillan telling his new player that a house was ready and waiting for him on the outskirts of Derby – a shrewd move since the manager knew Billy was hoping to marry within a few months. Keeping a highly-suspicious press corps in the dark, Billy, his fiancée Miss Lillian Dickie, of Ibrox, Glasgow, McMillan and his assistant manager Sammy Crooks made their way to Glasgow and thence by car to Derby. A night in a local hotel followed, and then an inspection of the house before the necessary forms were signed at the Baseball Ground. Only then were the newspapers called in.

Derby had got their man, and in the teeth of competition from no less a club than Liverpool, who, along with Middlesbrough, had reportedly made an offer of around £12,500. Billy was joining a club where two players – Tim Ward and Jack Howe – had been team-mates during the BAOR years.

Steel had a huge task ahead of him, having been bought to replace Peter Doherty, a legend at Derby who had moved to Huddersfield Town and who, along with Raich Carter, had been so instrumental in Derby's triumph in the FA Cup final of 1946 when they beat Charlton 4-1. How successful Billy was in clearing this hurdle will be touched on later, but how ironic that Billy's first home league match on 23 August was against Huddersfield, Peter Doherty et al! The game ended 0-0.

The 1948 clash between Scotland and England at Hampden on 10 April was won 2-0 by England despite their captain and right half, Billy Wright, being outmanoeuvred by Steel for most of the match. The result might have been different if, with the score at 1-0, a cross from Steel which found Delaney three yards out had been converted instead of being knocked past the post.

Billy recalled how, after the match, he incurred the wrath of skipper Young by chatting amicably to Stanley Matthews. George it seems, was not a good loser! In the absence of a team manager, the duties of Captain Young ran to organising travel, accommodation and even theatre tickets for his players.

Another tour of the Continent began on Saturday 22 May when Scotland pulverised Luxembourg, Steel scoring twice in the 6-1 win. The following day, in Paris, France beat Scotland 3-0, the experimental forward line of Rutherford (Rangers), Steel, Smith (Hibs), Charles Cox (Hearts) and David Duncan (East Fife), proving none too successful.

Later in the year, on 17 November, the Scots staged a marvellous recovery against Northern Ireland in Belfast. Having gone 2-0 down in the first five minutes, they fought back to secure a 3-2 win, the winner coming in the final minute from Billy Houliston. Steel played his part, being a constant threat throughout the match.

I became an even greater fan of Steel after *hearing* him play in the match against England on 9 April 1949. 'And it's Waddell, racing away...' intoned BBC radio commentator Peter Thomson as howls from 100,000 throats filled the living room of the family home at Broughty Ferry that sunny Saturday afternoon. It was Wembley's biggest-ever crowd. I sat enthralled beside our huge German wireless set, which had miraculously survived a journey home from the Rhineland in 1945, tucked under my dad's right arm.

Scotland took the Auld Enemy apart in an achievement of staggering proportions. England had lost just once since the war, to Scotland at Hampden in the 1946 Victory international when Delaney scored the only goal of the game. That encounter was not deemed a full international and no player was awarded a cap.

England had at their disposal men of the calibre of Matthews, Finney, Wright, Stan Mortensen, Mannion and Newcastle's Jackie Milburn. For my money they were, man for man, considerably better than the England of today. But Scotland were not to be denied, scoring through Jimmy Mason, Steel and Reilly. England's late counter came from Milburn. Steel helped to make Mason's goal in what was Scotland's first real attack. A radar-like pass found Reilly and the resultant cross from the winger allowed Mason to score from 12 yards. The time: 29 minutes. The youngest man on the park, twenty-year-old Reilly, remembers the goal very well. 'The ball struck Jimmy on the shin and crept in after hitting a post.'

The second half was but a few minutes old when Steel scored Scotland's second after a brilliant solo burst, then a pass to Houliston who collided with Swift. With both on the ground, Steel had the simplest task of rolling the ball home. Reilly's goal was the best of the three, a spectacular diving header from a Waddell cross after he had drifted into the centre-forward position.

Several head-to-head confrontations had a critical bearing upon the result that day. Left back Sammy Cox, whose position for Rangers was left half, had clearly done his homework on Matthews. He never left the Englishman's side all afternoon, knowing how he liked to have the ball played to his feet, not in front of him like most wingers. Matthews never got time to control the ball and faded into unaccustomed anonymity.

On the other side of the pitch Willie Waddell, also of Rangers, showed he had the beating of John Aston, the Manchester United left back and was a constant threat down the right side. Goalkeeper Jimmy Cowan had the toughest task – he took on the entire England forward line and during the first twenty minutes produced a series of breathtaking saves which, as Young put it later, broke the hearts of the home side.

Finally, there was Billy Steel. Busy helping out his defence in the early part of the match, Steel came into his own as Scotland began to penetrate the English rearguard, both he and Mason 'taking the game to a higher level,' to quote *The Times* of 11 April.

Steel was a will o' the wisp as Wright, the fierce-tackling Wolverhampton Wanderer, strove in vain to come to grips with him for the second year in a row. Centre forward Houliston had been selected specifically to upset that rock of the England defence, the imperturbable Neil Franklin of Stoke City. Houliston did his job well, harrying the centre half into several uncharacteristic errors.

Houliston had benefited from some sound advice on Franklin from Scotland reserve centre Willie Thornton, who, in his last encounter with the English, had tried to match Franklin skill for skill. 'It didn't work,' said Thornton. 'You go out and do exactly the opposite.'

Thornton also reminded Houliston that Franklin had always con-sidered another Scot - Jimmy Delaney - as the most difficult player he had ever had to deal with and Delaney was cast in the Houliston mould, strong, bustling, full of physical presence.

I can still reel off that Scotland team: Cowan (Morton); Young (Rangers), Cox (Rangers); Evans (Celtic), Woodburn (Rangers), Aitken (East Fife); Waddell (Rangers), Mason (Third Lanark), Houliston (Queen of the South), Steel (Derby County), Reilly (Hibs).

The left-wing partnership of Steel and Reilly had revealed itself to be an ace in the Scotland pack and Steel would refer to Reilly throughout his career as the best winger he had ever played with, although Reilly's international position from this point on would be mostly centre-forward. Reilly, still spry today in his mid-seventies, thought he could pin down the reason for Billy's appreciative comment.

'We'd swap positions,' he said. 'Billy would go to outside left, I would play inside left for a spell. It meant he didn't have to do the same amount of running about!' (Inside forwards and wing halves were the hardest working players on the park.)

Billy referred to this exchanging of positions in the chapter entitled 'Attack' in his book, giving as an example the case of one league team, before the war, which practised a method of preserving the energy of their inside forwards.

For the first twenty minutes the attack played in the customary formation, then the wingers and their inside partners changed roles. Not only did this tend to give the inside forwards a breather, it presented opposing defenders with a different problem to solve.

Another way to confuse defenders, according to Billy, was to initiate a double centre forward plan. 'In one big game,' as he put it, 'I was to lie back and our inside right had to stay in his normal position until I got the ball. My pass was to the centre forward, not in his usual position but when he had moved across the left side of the field between the right-back and the centre half. As he moved across I passed the ball and he received it roughly close to the 18-yard line, but over to the left.

'The centre half naturally followed him, leaving the middle of the park practically free of defenders. The only one left to cover that area was the left-back, who also had to keep an eye on the outside right.

'The centre forward, getting the ball, did not stop it but flicked it first time into the position he had just left, that wide open space. As the centre forward flicked the ball, it was the inside right's cue to move and he raced into this space to meet the ball. He had a running start on the left half covering him and even if the left-back came across to cover him, there was still the outside right there, ready to accept a pass. This move brought quite a few goals that day.'

There were occasions when Billy's tactical thinking could take a less formal shape as Reilly revealed another element in the secret of Scotland's success that April day in 1949. The Scots had been booked into the Oatlands Park Hotel, Weybridge, Surrey and Reilly recalled the team talk there the day before the game. George Young said: 'Billy, you are the only Anglo–Scot in the side. You play against these guys every week. What's our best approach?' Billy replied: 'Jist gie me the ba' and Ah'll tear them tae bits!'

It's a matter of history that this brave promise burst into full, rewarding flower and it was also a very rewarding reception Reilly got from his workmates when he turned up on the Monday morning to resume his job as a painter and decorator in Edinburgh.

The Hibs star went on to become perhaps the most instinctive goalscorer ever to appear in a Scotland jersey. Searingly quick off the mark, he was a two-footed player who, despite not being a tall man, was also superb in the air – not unlike Henrik Larsson in the Celtic team of today. In post-war football his strike rate of 22 goals in 38 games for his country has never been matched, not even by Denis Law. Reilly always seemed at his very best against England, who regarded him as absolutely lethal – he scored five times in his five appearances at Wembley – but Lawrie also had a healthy regard for the ability of the English.

'From time to time Scotland might have had a weakness in the odd position,' he said, 'but England were just so strong right throughout their teams.'

Scotland's victory secured the International Championship, which they had not won since 1936. And they did it without dropping a point. Just how well the Scots had played at Wembley was emphasised within a month, when England beat both Argentina and Portugal, at Wembley and at Goodison Park, Liverpool. The Scots were on a real roll. At Hampden on Wednesday 27 April they beat a very good French side 2-0 before 125,168 spectators. The report on the game by Jack Harkness in *The Courier & Advertiser* pinpointed the reason for Scotland's success.

'This has to be Billy Steel's finest-ever game in a football jersey. He was the only player at Hampden who could have scored the two goals which won the game. Goal number one: Billy found himself in a direct line with goalkeeper Vignal, who placed himself for the obvious right-foot shot. Billy slickly changed feet and lofted the ball over the bemused 'keeper's head with his left. Goal number two: A rocket from 20 yards, a knee-high thunderbolt that flashed under the body of the diving 'keeper.'

Harkness, a former Scotland goalkeeper, went on to praise the French who, 'in speed and first-time passing were well ahead but the forwards refused to shoot. Had Steel been in this French front rank, I shudder to think what would have happened.'

Now the Scots were due to collect the 'bonus' they had been promised for winning the International Championship – a 'once in a lifetime' tour to the United States and Canada. During May 1949 the players boarded the *Queen Mary* at Southampton, heading for New York. Also aboard were Newcastle United, at the start of *their* tour. The Geordies were not at all happy when they discovered the Scots were travelling second class while they had to make do with tourist class!

Just one match was lost in America, but what a defeat it was! In a game the Scots ought to have won about 10-0, the Irish club side Belfast Celtic beat the full Scottish international XI by 2-0 on a heavily-rutted pitch at Triborough Stadium, New York.

The party travelled throughout the United States by train, playing at venues like Philadelphia, Fall River and St Louis, where the floodlights were so poor the players could easily make out the stars.

In Canada, the Scots played in Toronto and Montreal. Before the Montreal match against East Canada, a huge party of exiled Scots, all carrying banners and Scottish emblems, broke down the dressing room door where the Scots were changing and shook the players' hands until they were sore!

The tour ended with a 5-0 win over the American national side in New York. Back in the British Isles, Scotland's great year continued with an 8-2 hammering of Northern Ireland at Windsor Park, Belfast on 1 October. It was noted that the strength of the Scots lay at wing half and at inside forward. Mention was made of the understanding of the players – Evans, Mason, Aitken and Steel. They provided ample openings for Reilly, Morris (East Fife) and Waddell. Steel scored the third goal. The thickset Morris, who scored a hat-trick, must have wondered what he had done wrong for he was never selected for Scotland again. It certainly seemed strange, yet emphasised the depth of forward talent available to the selectors at the time.

And the Windsor Park magic carried over into the match against Wales when Scotland won 2-0 at Hampden on 9 November. 'Star of the home side was undoubtedly Steel,' wrote *The Scotsman's* reporter in the issue of 10 November. 'He dominated play in a way no other player could approach. With Reilly he made up Scotland's most dangerous wing.'

The man from *The Scotsman* went on to describe Steel as 'a human dynamo of energy and skill. He invariably had the Welsh defence in a flurry.'

In terms of post-war football, 1949 represented Scotland's finest hour. The record was Played 4, Won 4, Goals For 15, Goals Against 3.

During February 1950, it was becoming obvious that something of a rift was developing between Steel and Derby County.

Billy was now living in Glasgow and training with Rangers at Ibrox Park, travelling south only when he had to – to play for his club. Sometimes he would not arrive before midnight on the Friday night. This arrangement incurred the displeasure of his team-mates and of Stuart McMillan, who nevertheless knew the value of his star forward. To try to hold onto Steel, Derby offered him a new two-year contract, with both club and player confirming that Steel had not asked for a transfer. Rumours persisted however, that the 'wee wizard' was about to become a Ranger.

On the other side of Scotland, Dundee Football Club were beginning to have goal-scoring problems. In their match against Raith Rovers on 10 April the Fifers won 4-1, Dundee's forwards looking distinctly shot-shy. On 11 May, on their own pitch, Dundee succumbed 3-0 to Celtic before a crowd of 11,000, the Dundonian element leaving the ground in a state of some disgruntlement.

Steel, despite the deteriorating situation at Derby, was continuing to win rave notices for his performances on the international scene. On Wednesday 26 April, he bewitched 123,751 people at Hampden in a match won by Scotland, the 3-1 victors over Switzerland. A real heartbreaker followed however, against England at the same venue. With six minutes to go, Scotland were 1-0 down through a goal by Roy Bentley when a subtle pass from Steel put centre forward Willie Bauld in the clear. From about 10 yards the Hearts man crashed the ball against the underside of the bar, only to watch in disbelief as it rebounded into play.

In the final international of the season Billy took part in Scotland's 1-0 win over France in Paris on 29 May, the only goal coming from East Fife's Alan Brown. A week earlier the Scots, with Steel in his usual berth at inside left, had drawn 2-2 with Portugal in Lisbon.

Turning the clock back, in his column in the *Sporting Post* of 29 April, Rambler quoted an un-named star, then with an English club and plainly discontented with his lot. The mystery man said: 'I wish I'd had someone to advise me before I decided to leave Scotland. I am sure that I would have been as well off if I had gone to a good Scottish club.' In England, he said, he could earn no more than £12 a week, plus bonuses. 'In Scotland I could have got the same, plus a job if I wanted one.' Steel sparked off frantic speculation when he turned up to watch the Rangers-Dundee match on Saturday 16 September. It was noted that he had got to Ibrox aboard the Dundee team bus.

The event re-ignited a seemingly lifeless issue — the transfer of Steel to Dundee, whose offer of £18,000 during August to Derby

County had been turned down as 'not nearly enough'. Derby had been holding out for £25,000. Steel dampened down the excitement by saying he had no idea what football held in store for him. He was anticipating opening a shop in Glasgow within two months (he did eventually open a sports outfitters shop in the city).

It was beginning to look like Steel would be lost to football forever. Certainly he no longer appeared to be part of Derby's plans. When the club resumed their season in the English First Division in August, Steel's name was noticeable by its absence from the team sheet. Billy was on the way out.

-3-
Derby to Dundee

Although he had taken time to settle at Derby, it is fair to say that he eventually succeeded in winning over a sceptical home support. For the first two months, according to Derby fan Arthur Sims of Belper, he struggled to find his feet but then, at Anfield on 25 October, he dominated the game against Liverpool and scored two wonder goals in the 2-2 draw there.

'After that,' said Arthur, 'he could do no wrong and was absolutely worshipped by the Derby fans. He formed a brilliant partnership with Raich Carter. After Carter left, several players were tried to play alongside Billy but then Derby again broke the transfer record by paying £24,500 for Johnny Morris from Manchester United, who formed a great partnership with Steel.'

Lifelong Derby fan Len Stringer from the Allenton area of the town remembers Billy as having 'that touch of class. He could produce some wonderful bursts of speed, putting the opposing wing half the wrong way. Many opponents resorted to 'the heavy stuff', but Billy could give as good as he got, especially with people as hard as Jimmy Scoular of Portsmouth [a fellow Scot] and the Aston Villa hard men of that era.'

Among Derby fans' best memories of the era would have been the match against Arsenal at the Baseball Ground on 29 November 1947, which ended the Gunners' unbeaten run of 17 games. Steel and Carter were in devastating form on a day which saw 36,605 take in the match. Derby's 1-0 win moved them to third spot in the league.

Another unforgettable occasion, recalled by Maurice Holland of Belper, took place at Maine Road where Manchester City went into the dressing room at half-time 3-1 up.

'After that, Billy just took over,' said Maurice. 'I seem to remember we ran out winners by 5-3.'

R. Teece, of Chesterfield, wrote: 'Little Billy Steel was a pleasure to watch, I believe one of the greatest I have ever seen. What a partnership with Raich Carter! What would be their worth now?'

Clive Williamson of Spondon, Derby spoke of Billy as 'this wonderful, marvellous player'.

A contemporary *Stanley Matthews Football Album* seemed to agree. Within its pages Billy was described as 'the cleverest inside forward of today'.

The same publication however, contained advice from Carter on Inside Forward Play, during which he named several great men he had played with and against. There was no reference to Steel. And in Billy's book, Carter is conspicuous by his absence from the list of players the author gives as excelling in their arts – men like Matthews, Mannion and Doherty. Carter and Steel undoubtedly had something of a problem.

Ex-Dens Parker George Hill recalls being in Hull with Tommy Gallacher when they spotted a shop owned by Raich Carter.

'We went in to have a look round,' recalled George 'and Carter came out from behind the counter, spotted our club blazers and said: "Dundee boys...how's that little b... Steel?"'

According to the England legend, Billy had lost no time in telling him how to play the game!

Carter moved to Hull City in the 1948/49 season and it may have been no coincidence that Billy was Derby's joint top-scorer that year with 14 goals. That season proved to be a remarkable one in the history of English football. FA figures for spectators showed an all-time record – 41 million fans paid to watch league and cup fixtures.

The diminutive Scot was accused by some players at Derby of being difficult to play with but this was by no means a universal view. For instance, Lawrie Reilly, who represented Scotland many times with Billy, described him as being 'a treat to play with'.

However, another Derby fan, Frank Broomhead of Mickleover, who had watched his team play for about seventy years, said of Billy: 'His temperament was his big problem, not his football. Great player though he was, Billy never achieved greatness at Derby.'

Frank was able to supply a few statistics from Billy's spell there. He scored 27 goals in 109 league matches and 8 in 15 FA Cup appearances.

Some of the Scot's difficulties at the Baseball Ground may indeed have been down to his temperament for there *is* evidence that he could be impatient with others less able than himself. But it seems clear it was mainly the 'star status' awarded to him by the club which did not endear him to the rest of the playing staff, some of whom resented the fact that he earned money by means other than playing football. There were even suggestions of illegal payments associated with Billy's alleged sessions in management training in the club president's store in Derby.

Team-mates also accused him of not trying in some matches and talked of 'kidding' him into turning on the magic by mentioning on the way to the ground that the secretary of the Scottish Football Association, George Graham, would be in the crowd that day!

Billy's final game for Derby came on 5 May 1950, when the Rams beat Bolton Wanderers 4-0. He was, according to Arthur Sims, 'never to be forgotten by those of us who saw him play for Derby. A truly great player'.

Even after his departure from the club he was blamed for the subsequent decline in the fortunes of Derby. This seems uncharitable, considering the huge profit they made on selling him. It is also worth asking what the reaction of those players would have been in the event of their being offered the same status as Steel. Would they, for the sake of the club, have turned down such divisive temptations? I am content to leave it to the reader to answer that one.

Billy watched the Rangers-Dundee match end in a 0-0 draw which served to emphasise the continuing problem the Taysiders were having in finding the net. Indeed, although the season was but a few weeks old, they had already fielded ten forwards. Four days later Dundee FC signed Billy Steel for a then record sum for any Scottish player − £23,500. It is a measure of the value placed upon Steel that the record figure was not surpassed for another ten years.

Dundee's manager, George Anderson, having failed to land Steel with the much-publicised bid in August, had travelled south in secret this time to negotiate the fee with Derby and he announced his new signing at a press conference on 21 September.

Steel's decision to opt for Dundee had hinged very much on what he thought of Anderson. In an article written for the Dundee Supporters Club annual, Billy revealed that it was the kindness of the director-manager which lured him to Dens.

He wrote: 'One of the luckiest days of my football career was a Sunday when I stepped into a high-powered Super Snipe limousine in George Square, Glasgow, and met a man attired in bow tie and bowler hat.

'No doubt all Dundee fans recognise that I refer to Mr George Anderson. If it had not been for him I would probably have been an Aberdeen player because that very morning I had spoken to Mr David Halliday of Aberdeen about signing for the Dons.

'I remembered Mr Anderson from his Aberdeen days when I played with the Army teams who visited Pittodrie and I remembered his kindness on these occasions.

'One day in particular will always remain with me when I was up at reveille in Edinburgh, caught the ten o' clock train for Aberdeen, rushed to Linksfield in the town and took part in a five-a-side competition. Our five were Jimmy Carabine, Tommy Walker, Bobby

Campbell, George Sutherland and myself, all Signals men stationed in Edinburgh. After collecting the first prize of national savings certificates at 5 p.m., we caught a train out of Aberdeen ten minutes later. This was accomplished with the aid of a taxi driver who had no respect for human life.

'Entering the platform we anticipated a miserable journey until Mr Anderson appeared and led us to a reserved compartment which contained two boxes, one filled with sandwiches and fruit, the other containing lemonade and, to Jimmy Carabine's delight, a plentiful supply of Guinness.

'The conversation for the next few miles centred on Mr Anderson and the boys agreed it was a halo he should wear instead of a bowler. Result was I decided Dundee was the place for me.'

Billy went on to say he wished he had joined Dundee some years earlier. 'Dundee has a small-town spirit or clanishness,' he wrote. 'It gives a player the feeling of having an interest instead of being just one of a very large number. I've had some great experiences since coming to the Jute City.'

Now the man with the size 5 boots was on my very doorstep. Dundee were aware of the plans he had for Glasgow, where he also would be allowed to train.

Although none knew it then, Steel could lay claim to be the only person to have played at Dens Park for one minute! He came on as an 89th-minute substitute for the Army team which played Dundee in the testimonial match for the late Bob McGlashan in 1946.

Asked by the press what it felt like to be a £23,500 player, the self-assured Steel said: 'Nothing to it. I'm used to this sort of thing. When I left Morton I needed a suitcase to carry my share of the fee!'

The acquisition of Steel would turn out to be the biggest coup ever pulled off by manager Anderson yet he had to face virulent criticism for signing for such a staggering figure a player who was clearly out of condition and who had not played a competitive match for many a moon. When it became known that Steel would be pitchforked into Saturday's game against Aberdeen, the doom-mongers had a field day, forecasting calamity against an in-form Pittodrie side. It would be Steel's first game for six months and the barrackers among the local support, notorious both for the volume of their disapproval and for their ignorance of the game, began to tune up their tonsils. Dens Park was bursting at the seams for the match, 34,000 fans having almost fought their way in.

The would-be critics had to spend the full 90 minutes in total silence. Steel, showing master touches all afternoon, scored the first goal from 15 yards in the 71st minute to a roar that might have lifted the Dens Road buses off their wheels. It was a winning debut in which he cleverly managed to disguise his relative lack of fitness. As he left the dressing room after the game, Steel was besieged by autograph hunters.

Dundee's next match, against Morton, was eagerly awaited by both sets of fans. Both teams were undefeated in the league and Steel of course was a former Morton man. The match, on 30 September at Greenock, was played in a downpour which taxed the stamina of every man on the park.

With 20 minutes to go, Dundee looked dead and buried. They were 2-0 down but Steel, who ought to have been the least fit man on view, now took the game by the scruff of the neck, dragging the ball past defender after defender to set up chances for his team-mates.

He himself scored the equaliser before and, with just five minutes to go, he quickly controlled the ball well out from the home penalty box, looked up and began to work his way forward. He beat two defenders then lost the ball, immediately regained possession and beat another man before teeing it up for left-winger Jimmie Andrews, who was pulled down in the act of shooting – penalty! Skipper Alf Boyd, formerly a ball boy at Dens, scored the winner from the spot.

In the manner of all their kind, the prophets of doom from a couple of weeks previously now melted away, somehow managing to overlook just how wrong they had been. The *People's Journal* football correspondent, Unomi, in the 7 October issue, highlighted a little-known aspect of the Steel persona.

'I have to hand it to Steel for his courtesy and patience,' wrote Unomi. 'On Monday [2 October] at Beechwood and Tannadice parks, he signed hundreds of autographs. No one was refused.'

When Billy was selected to play for Scotland against Wales at Cardiff on 21 October, he was the first Dundee player to be capped since Colin McNab played against England in April 1932. This physical encounter in front of 60,000 fans ended in victory for Scotland by 3-1, the visitors' goals coming from Reilly (2) and Liddell.

In the next international, on 1 November, against Ireland at Hampden, Steel was head and shoulders above everyone else on the park in Scotland's 6-1 win. One tabloid carried the headline Steel 6, Ireland 1. In fact, Billy scored four that day, all in the second half, against a team which included Peter Doherty. Steel's goal in the 53rd minute was a tribute to the speed of his reactions. In the act of shooting he slipped and landed on his back. Before anyone could move he was on his feet again and drove a fierce left-foot shot into the net.

The Scotsman of 2 November reported: 'There was nothing to equal Steel's dazzling and darting runs, each one fraught with danger for the Irishmen.'

Billy's was the best scoring performance by any Scot in a full international since Hughie Gallacher notched five against Ireland in 1929. The *Sporting Post*'s football correspondent, Rambler, referred to Steel's display as 'the best I have seen for years.'

Alf Boyd, congratulating his team-mate on his performance, asked: 'When are you going to score four for us, Billy?'

Billy did not score four in Dundee's next game against Partick Thistle at Dens on 28 October, but he did haul his side back into it as half-time approached, with the visitors two goals up. Steel worked his way through 'in delightful fashion' to finish off the move with a daisy-cutter from 20 yards. Steel continued in top gear during the second half and the Dens Parkers came out ahead by 3-2. They were top of the league with 12 points, having played 8, won 5, lost 1 and drawn 2.

Dundee visited Stark's Park, Kirkcaldy, on the following Saturday, a daunting venue in those days, and came away with a 1-0 victory. It was a fiercely contested match and served admirably to demonstrate another Steel asset – his strength. In the course of a bruising run in the 50th minute, he rode three bone-crunching tackles before hammering in a shot that had 'goal' written all over it until Rovers' left half Andy Leigh hurled himself into its path.

Dundee took on St Mirren at Dens on Saturday 25 November and scored five without reply. Steel was in world-class form. Unomi considered Steel's performance as 'the finest exhibition of football skill seen at Dens for many a day. He never had the ball off the carpet and the things he did with it were nobody's business.'

On 9 December at Bayview, Methil, which had been something of a graveyard for Dundee in the past, the visitors won 2-0, the highlight of the game being a 50-yard run by Steel. He was the only Scotland forward to catch the eye during the 1-0 defeat by Austria at a frost-bound Hampden on 12 December – the first time Scotland had lost a home match to Continental opposition, albeit to a team which was then considered the best in Europe. The Scots were astonished by the Austrian defensive tactics, which seemed to consist largely of handling the ball provided it was outside their penalty area. Their skipper had to be told through a translator that this was not acceptable in Scottish football!

Three days later at Airdrie, Dundee won 3-0, Steel scoring twice, both goals, according to the *Courier & Advertiser* of 11 December, carrying 'the stamp of the master'.

The next match against Rangers at Dens was won 2-0 by Dundee, a scoreline which neither reflected their superiority nor provided any hint of the masterclass given by Steel that day. The team's success was put down in part to the Continental-style rubber boots worn by the players – believed to be the first time they had been tried in Scotland.

On 23 December, at Tynecastle, Hearts held the league leaders to a 1-1 draw but only a save in a thousand by 'keeper Jimmy Brown prevented a Steel thunderbolt from putting the visitors ahead. (Steel had once guested for Hearts, during 1944.)

-4-
Triumph and Adversity

1950 saw Billy Steel's one chance to play in the World Cup finals vanish in incomprehensible fashion. Scotland, having qualified for the tournament in Brazil by coming second in the Home International Championship, decided not to take part. It would have been the first time Scotland competed in the event.

The England players all found themselves asked the same question during their time in Brazil: 'Why did the Scots not come?'

Sports journalists could not fathom why the SFA had declined their invitation to the World Cup either.

John Graydon of Kemsley Newspapers, who covered the tournament for *The Times*, was certain the Scots would have done well where England had only managed to deliver what were described as 'a series of lame performances'.

'Scotland has perfected the art of combining clever but progressive football. Their forwards do not flatter to deceive.

'Unlike so many teams in the World Cup, they could call upon wingers in Billy Liddell and Willie Waddell who never hesitate to cut in and have a shot. Only on rare occasions did I see wingers have a crack at goal. Defences showed up badly when this happened.

'The Scotland team I saw at Hampden [against England] was a sounder, all-round combination than England took to Rio.'

Many Scots living in Brazil had taken their holidays to coincide with the World Cup and were devastated by the SFA decision, for which no believable reason has ever surfaced. For the record, Uruguay beat Brazil in the final.

19 January 1951 saw Dundee stage a superb comeback against a rampant Celtic side at Dens. 1-0 down at half-time, the home team took the fight to Celtic and 'fight' is the right word. Billy Steel was flattened time after time but kept coming up smiling and laid on every Dundee goal in a 3-1 win before 28,000 fans.

Now the city of Dundee found itself shaking with excitement in anticipation of the first round Scottish Cup tie between Dundee and Dundee United, whose paths seldom crossed, United being a B Division outfit. As the build-up to the match continued, the *Courier & Advertiser* pointed out that United had just one problem to solve – what to do about Steel. The warning was not lost on United. They did what most other teams through bitter experience had already learned to do – detailed two men to keep him quiet. It worked. During the match on 26 January, Steel hardly got a kick at the ball and it served to illustrate the difficulties faced by all players of such class. To combat this constant close attention, Steel had tried to get into the habit of playing the ball first time. 'Tee up the ball for a pass or a shot and you'll lose it,' he said.

Billy also tried to get into the habit when shooting of concentrating on direction rather than power but as any fan who had seen him play would undoubtedly confirm, he generally was able to produce both!

38,000 spectators paid a total of £2,850, excluding stand and enclosure fees, to watch the tie end in a 2-2 draw and in the replay on Wednesday 31 January, all United's careful planning for Billy came to nought when he scored the only goal of the game. After the match, the Dundee star teased United about the goal, which he had scored from 30 yards, by claiming that he had 'put screw on the ball' to deceive goalkeeper Wyllie.

On 10 February, Dundee visited Perth on league business to play St Johnstone, for whom centre forward Paddy Buckley was in deadly form. Thousands were waiting outside the ground long before the turnstiles opened at 1.40 p.m., 1 hour and 20 minutes before kick-off. This Tayside derby attracted 29,972 and ended with Dundee winning 3-1.

With the international against England in mind, due to take place in April, the chairman of the Scottish selectors, Walter Johnstone, took in the Motherwell/Dundee game at Fir Park on 17 February. Dundee won 2-0 and the chairman saw Steel in his most impish mood, continually carving out openings from seemingly impossible situations and Mr Johnstone said after the match: 'I am delighted to have been able to attend such an exhibition.'

There can be no doubt that the presence of Steel in the Dundee side added greatly to the gate even for run-of-the-mill matches. Dundee's fourth round Scottish Cup clash with Raith Rovers at Dens was a case in point. The crowd was an official record, 40,920 having compressed themselves into the ground. Dundee lost 2-1.

Despite the plus points, it was not all sweetness and light at Dens. Billy was beginning to irritate his team-mates by constantly shouting for the ball and not being backward about showing his feelings when he didn't get it! George Anderson called a meeting of the players to clear the air and shocked most of them by siding with Steel, accusing the others of being jealous. The manager's instruction? Lay off!

It was said of the Scottish selectors at the time that when picking a team, Steel's name was the first they put down. Billy provided no reason for doubting this when he starred in Scotland's 3-2 win at Wembley on Saturday 14 April.

Reilly, Steel and Billy Liddell were Scotland's outstanding players in a game which was somewhat marred by an injury to Wilf Mannion, who suffered a fractured cheekbone in an aerial clash with Liddell in the 13th minute. With no substitutes allowed, England had to carry on with ten men. However, the Scots had already served notice that they meant business. Their forwards had two phases of concentrated brilliance – the first fifteen minutes of each half.

The Times of 16 April wrote: 'Steel, who was Scotland's general in attack, was quick to detect a flaw at the heart of England's defensive works. At once, as if at his invisible signal, Scotland began to play on Jack Froggatt at centre half.'

It paid off, the Portsmouth pivot being constantly pulled out of position and although England rallied bravely, they could not find a final equaliser. However, Steel had to turn up on his own goal line to block a shot from Finney which would have given England the draw. It was, said *The Times*, 'a magnificent struggle of skill and excitement'.

Scotland had won the International Championship again with the following record: Played 3, Won 3, Drawn 0, Lost 0. The Scots notched up 12 goals and lost 4, which was by far the best scoring record of any of the home countries.

The next international against the all-amateur Danish side at Hampden on 12 May resulted in a 3-1 win for the Scots, Steel scoring 'a dandy goal' with his head. No one knew it then, but that was destined to be Billy's last-ever goal in a full international.

He played in the next, on 17 May, when the Scots beat France 1-0 in a turgid match at Hampden, not one single Scottish forward managing to distinguish himself.

A brief Continental tour was now undertaken by a Scotland party, conducted by road and ferry after the previous tour's near miss at Brussels airport. Scotland's first match against Belgium on Sunday 20 May, saw the Scottish forwards in irresistible form, especially George Hamilton of Aberdeen, who scored wonderful a hat-trick, the last goal being created by Steel.

It is worthy of note that Hamilton, who was so nervous that he had hardly slept a wink the night before the match, was considered by John Graydon to have given the best centre-forward performance he had seen since Tommy Lawton was at his best. As though to emphasise the depth of talent available to the Scotland selectors at that time, George Young also named Hamilton in his short list of the best players he had ever faced. Yet the Aberdeen craftsman was never an automatic choice for the national side.

In Vienna, a week after the Belgium game, the visitors were put to the sword by the Austrians, the militaristic phrase being particularly apt. Austria outclassed Scotland 4-0, but in the process they incurred the contempt of every sports writer with the visiting party.

The Courier & Advertiser's special correspondent wrote of 'the most degrading exhibition of football I have ever witnessed. The second half was nothing more than a common street brawl. I have never been more ashamed of the game of football.'

Referee Lutz of Switzerland came in for bitter criticism, habitually turning a blind eye to quite cynical violence from the home side. In the 82nd minute Steel was sent off for an alleged foul on centre half Ocwirk. This sublimely skilled defender ruined a great display by histrionic writhings all over the turf as Steel got his marching orders. Billy was the first Scot in living memory to be sent off in a full international.

George Young happened to be watching Steel closely, for the little man had been kicked continuously throughout the match. 'From my position, close to the incident, I saw no foul committed. His being sent off was a humiliating experience he did not deserve.'

The tone for match had been set in the very first minute when Waddell went past the opposing full-back only to find himself lifted off his feet and thrown six feet over the touchline. George Hamilton, who ended the game a mass of bruises, was given offside while a full-back stood on the Austrian goal line.

Two of the Austrian training staff frequently appeared on the pitch handing out slices of lemon to their players. 'The skin from this fruit just littered the pitch by the end of the match,' Young recalled.

After the game, Young immediately sought out Steel, who was under the shower. 'Don't worry, Billy,' he said 'we are all with you.' 'It's good of you to say that skipper,' Billy replied, 'for I'm very fed up.'

The chairman of the selection committee, Walter Johnstone, and George Graham came into the dressing room and made it clear they would be taking no action against Steel.

Even the post-match get-together by the players of both sides turned into a farce for at dinner that evening the Austrians completely ignored their visitors.

'I began to wonder,' wrote Young of that sad day for sport, 'if international football matches do always make for international friendship and understanding. In Vienna the Austrian team did nothing to make us want to meet them again on the football field.'

Four years later, when Scotland returned to the Prater Stadium, Vienna to play the Austrians on 19 May 1955, another massacre seemed on the cards. Austria had recently drawn with the fabulous Hungarians. (It must surely be worth noting that like Brazil in a later era, all football came to be judged by the standards the Hungarians set. The Magical Magyars, as they were called, changed the face of world football forever in the space of six months. Although they had already earned a great reputation before their match against England on 25 November 1953, this was the contest which propelled them into the global limelight.) The Scots had been mauled by England 7-2 at Wembley just weeks before, partly on account of a nightmare performance by 'keeper Fred Martin of Aberdeen. However, Scotland played a fluent passing game throughout the 90 minutes in Vienna, this time managing to rise above yet another brutal display by the home side and ran out winners by 4 goals to 1. It may have been the most amazing result ever achieved by a Scotland team abroad – it was certainly greater in terms of degree of difficulty than any of the Wembley wins – and it was a major triumph for their captain, Gordon Smith.

England had never lost a game to Continental opposition on their own turf and although none was in any doubt that the Hungarians, champions of the 1952 Helsinki Olympics, would provide a stiff test, there was no lack of confidence in the England camp.

It is a matter of record that Hungary beat England 6–3 but what can never be found in the record books is any reference to the manner of that defeat. England were overwhelmed by a display of soccer artistry the likes of which no one at Wembley had ever seen before, played as it happened, by a team who at the same time introduced the game to short football shorts!

Using a system which incorporated a deep-lying centre forward in the person of Nandor Hidegkuti of the Red Banner club, the Hungarians played a kind of total football almost twenty years before the Dutch imagined they invented it.

They combined the short-passing game of the Continentals with the long pass from midfield, always struck, it seemed, at precisely the right moment in front of their flying wingers. The England defenders, already struggling to cope with the subtle skills of inside forwards Sandor Kocsis and Ferenc Puskas and wingmen Budai and Czibor, were thrown into a panic every time. Hidegkuti launched himself into the penalty box, sometimes from as distant a location as the centre circle, a red-shirted streak whose position on the field today might be likened to that of an attacking midfield player. He scored a hat-trick.

Puskas, the better-known of the inside forwards, was dubbed 'The Galloping Major' and went on to have a glittering career with Real Madrid. Kocsis, however, may have been the more accomplished player. He was deadly in the air as one staggering statistic underlines: he scored with his head on one out of every three corners won by his side, Honved, during one domestic season in Hungary.

England's chance for revenge came on 23 May 1954 when they tackled the Hungarians at the People's Stadium, Budapest but they were now under no illusion about the scale of the task ahead. Hungary had not lost a game in their own country since 1945.

It would be unfair to England to say they had learned nothing from the humiliation of a few months ago. It was simply that the players who could have coped with the Hungarians were not available. The visitors suffered their heaviest-ever defeat (7-1) which would have been 8-1 had not the referee disallowed what seemed not only a genuine goal but one which had arrived at the end of a move of stunning precision.

One England player said after the match: 'I have never seen anything like it. They were men from another planet. The Hungarian attack, in all its imaginative conception, was like light passing through a prism.'

Part of the problem was that British football had become, in the words of Pozzo, the mastermind who piloted the Italian team to their new, lofty place in world football, 'utterly predictable'. He said: 'Continental teams can read British teams like an open book, as players behave in international matches absolutely the same as in league games; same moves; same tactics; same tendencies – all on one pattern.'

In searching for reasons why the Continentals had advanced so much while the British game stubbornly remained stuck in the same rut, it is worth noting that in Hungary the national side was given far higher priority than the club set-up.

Unfortunately, one reason for this had less to do with football than with the international prestige sought and bought through sport by regimes like Communist Hungary. But a good example of this dedication, however fuelled, came during 1954 when the World Cup was due to be played in Switzerland. That year the entire Hungarian domestic league season was cancelled, giving the international side a full six months to prepare for the tournament, which they ought to have won. 2-0 up in the final against West Germany, they somehow contrived to lose 3-2.

Even away from such prestigious events, the players did not always disband after each international but were usually kept together, training in intense spells of about an hour each at Margaret Island, Budapest. During these sessions not a word was spoken!

It remains one my great regrets that I never saw that team in action. They altered football completely, especially in Britain.

Those six months in which they destroyed England rang the death knell of the old 1, 2, 3, 5 system, sometimes called the WM system. A new, more tactical future had already arrived, although it is worth noting that the theory of the deep-lying centre forward was not unknown before the Hungarians tried it. The difference lay in the matchless calibre of the player they were able to deploy in that role.

-5-
Winning Ways

As part of Billy's 1951 summer schedule, Dundee engaged in a tour of Israel and Turkey, beginning in late May and ending when the party got back to Dundee on Tuesday 26 June. Billy and his team-mates brought back with them many a wonderful memory, plus another of a different kind – of the most blatantly partisan refereeing at every game played in Turkey. However, the players would have felt a warm glow from the news that their maximum weekly wage limit had just risen to £14.

When Dundee took part in a curtain-raiser for the new season on 14 July they went down 4-3 to Motherwell at Dens in the first round of the St Mungo Cup, a competition for A Division clubs, which was held by Glasgow Corporation to celebrate the Festival of Great Britain. Steel put in such a second half that he almost single-handedly silenced a group of slow handclappers who had seen Dundee go into the dressing room at half-time 4-1 down. Working like a Trojan, Steel tried to rally his team-mates. Having scored the only Dundee goal in the first half, he scored again in the 77th minute, and then beat three men in a mazy dribble before parting to Hill, who scored Dundee's third. 19,000 watched the action.

An altogether more prestigious competition was the Scottish League Cup, conducted in two sections. The winner of each played one another in the final. In the first match against St Mirren at Love Street, Paisley on 11 August, Dundee led 2-0 through goals by Toner and Flavell, but let the home side back into it and the match ended 2-2.

In the same competition a week later, Dundee thrashed Raith Rovers 5-0 at Dens in a match illuminated by Steel. In one bewildering run, Steel beat Leigh, and then Colville before hammering in a shot that was brilliantly saved by 'keeper Gray. The little man was not to be denied. In the 43rd minute Billy left the defence standing. Gray, coming out to meet him, could only watch in cringing embarassment as a delightful chip soared over his head and landed in the net. In the 53rd minute Steel struck a cunning pass into the path of Andrews who crossed for Toner to score.

Steel came in for some very rough treatment from the Raith defenders, who were now resorting to strong-arm tactics in an effort to contain him. But the 72nd minute saw another shrewd ball from Steel snapped up by Toner for his second goal and the centre got his hat-trick with five minutes to go, courtesy of another assist from Steel.

Quite unfairly, the fans began to expect this level of service from Steel all the time and it was indeed his distribution of the ball that helped to make him such compulsive viewing. He had the ability, like Varga in a later era, to pass without breaking his stride. It continually surprised the spectator, and presumably opposing players, to see the ball emerge smoothly from racing feet on its way to a team-mate.

Rangers' first visit of the season to Dens on 29 September drew a crowd of 31,000. For this league encounter, the visitors took to the field in an unfamiliar white strip. The game was only six minutes old when it burst into life with the kind of goal that would never be forgotten by any who witnessed it. There seemed little danger when Bobby Flavell passed to Steel thirty yards from goal, but without looking up Billy hit the ball first time with his left foot and it fairly hurtled into the top right-hand corner with 'keeper Bobby Brown clawing helplessly at thin air. The goal had 'Denny' written all over it, Steel's birthplace having furnished employment for Brown, a teacher of physical education at Denny High School.

The half-time summary by the *Sporting Post* described Steel's contribution as 'inspirational'. There was no more scoring and Billy would go on to miss the 6 October international against Ireland in Belfast, having limped off the pitch with a badly bruised ankle. That ankle would give him trouble for the remainder of his career.

Steel did not return to duty for Dundee until the semi-final of the League Cup at Motherwell on 13 October, but the 5-1 score-line in favour of Dundee was hardly a matter of coincidence. Steel's constant probing created near-panic in the home defence and he laid on goals for Christie, Pattillo and Flavell, who scored a hat-trick. In the other semi, a 'bang in form' Rangers side beat Celtic 3-0.

The omens as the final approached did not look good for Dundee, who had never won the cup. Rangers on the other hand, regarded the trophy almost as their own, having won it six times. However, there was a quiet confidence about the Dundee players, done no harm at all by their 2-1 defeat of Celtic on 20 October in a league match at Dens. The day of the final, 27 October, dawned bright and clear and Hampden was a sea of colour as 92,325 fans, most of them standing, settled down to watch this clash of the Glasgow giants, who fielded eight internationals that day, and the upstarts from the other side of the country.

It was, as with all finals in which Rangers took part, virtually a home game for them and the Light Blues began well. By the interval they were up 1-0 and it should have been more. Dundee came out for the second half firing on all cylinders and in just two minutes they had equalised through Flavell. They now entered upon a spell of ascendancy in which Steel almost knocked Bobby Brown off his feet with a ferocious drive before Johnny Pattillo put Dundee ahead in the 69th minute.

The game seemed to be petering out as Dundee held on with relative ease but in the 88th minute a Rangers free kick somehow eluded both Bill Brown in the Dundee goal and the Rangers centre Willie Thornton and slipped over the line – 2-2!

A minute later Steel was fouled and Dundee were awarded a free kick on the edge of the Rangers penalty area. Steel called to Boyd: 'I'll put it on your head, Alfie!'

The cross was inch perfect. At the far post Boyd rose majestically to head the winner. It was Dundee's first major trophy in forty years. Boyd was chaired off the pitch by Steel and Gallacher.

In the *Dundee Evening Telegraph* of the following Monday, Rambler wrote that he was promoting Steel from General to Field Marshal. It had been Steel, wrote Rambler, who regrouped a shaken Dundee side after Rangers opened the scoring.

The Scotsman of 29 October wrote: 'Steel had a magnificently inspiring game.'

When the victors returned to Dundee by train in the evening, 30,000 people were lining the streets to greet them.

Injury sidelined Billy from mid-November until mid-December and there were increasing worries about the condition of his left ankle. In that period Dundee did not win one single match. They lost again by 4-3 when he returned in a league encounter with Airdrie on 15 December but oh, how agonising the manner of going under! Airdrie were awarded two hotly-disputed penalties and converted both. Steel meantime was in prime form, covering the entire Broomfield pitch and spraying perfect passes to his mates. Billy scored Dundee's second and laid on the third for Flavell with 15 minutes to go. At Dens, on the following Saturday, Dundee romped home by 4-1 against Stirling Albion, Steel again pulling the strings.

With the start of a new year, the match everyone in Dundee and Edinburgh was looking forward to was the visit of Hearts in a league fixture at Dens. Both teams were in supreme form and the match on 5 January 1952 lived up to its star billing. I should know. I was there. Dundee had defeated Rangers 2-1 at Ibrox just three days before and there was some concern that they might pay the price in tired legs against Hearts. The match at Ibrox had been played on a strength-sapping pitch covered in two inches of snow and both skippers had pleaded in vain to have the fixture postponed.

However, Dundee's win was their first in a league match at Ibrox for 27 years and it was marked by a wonderful goal from Steel. Midway through the first half he collected the ball 30 yards out and curled a shot away from 'keeper Brown to enter the net via his left-hand post.

At that particular moment the challenge presented by Hearts looked even more daunting, their feared inside forward trio of Conn, Bauld and Wardhaugh striking terror into defences wherever they went.

A massive crowd saw Dundee start as though they meant to sweep the visitors into the River Tay. With Hill, Gallacher, Steel and Christie all in irrresistible mood, the home side were two up in 16 minutes. Steel scored the second, a goal that will live forever in the memory of all those lucky enough to have been there. Every detail remains etched upon my mind.

Steel had taken a pass in the area around the right-hand corner of Hearts' penalty box. As usual a cluster of defenders moved in quickly to close him down. Not the usual two, three this time, creating a seemingly impenetrable wall of maroon jerseys.

Steel feinted right then in the blink of an eye transferred both his weight and the ball to his left side and with no discernible backlift, sent a left-foot shot streaking just inside the goalkeeper's right-hand post. For a milli-second there was silence. It had all happened just too quickly. But then 32,000 throats roared as one in appreciation of a moment of pure footballing magic. Hearts weathered the storm and managed to pull one back. At half-time they must have been congratulating themselves on being just a goal behind. The second half was played out in complete contrast to the first. Now it was all Hearts and by the end Dundee, surely suffering from their efforts in mid-week, had to hang on doggedly for a draw.

Parkhead was Dundee's next port of call on league business on 19 January and although Celtic took a deserved lead, Steel responded in the 16th minute with a shot from 18 yards which 'ripped its way into the net.' Final score: 1-1.

On 9 February, Dundee faced a potential banana skin in the second round of the Scottish Cup. They had to make the long trip to Wigtown on the Solway Firth to take on the locals on their narrow, bumpy pitch at Crammonford Park. It had all the ingredients of a nightmare in the making but Steel in particular showed no mercy to the lower leaguers, scoring twice and laying on three more in a 7-1 rout, played out before a record crowd of 4,500.

Prior to the match, the Wigtown President had jokingly offered Billy half a dozen pies to slow him down!

Back to the bread-and-butter fare of the league and on 1 March, Dundee gave St Mirren a going over at Dens. The game, according to the *Sporting Post*'s minute-by-minute report, revealed Steel 'at his most tantalising'. He made the first goal when he romped past two defenders to place the ball in front of Burrell. Dundee cruised to a 3-0 victory.

The fourth round tie against Aberdeen at Dens on 8 March had the look of a cracker about it, but a Steel-inspired Dundee trounced the Dons 4-0. One move saw Billy trail Don after Don in his wake before parting to Burrell, whose goal was ruled offside. Steel needed no help in the 50th minute, weaving his way past several defenders then cracking home a beauty. He scored again in the 82nd minute.

Monday's issue of *The Scotsman* wrote: 'The decisive factors were the superiority of Dundee's wing halves, Gallacher and Boyd, and the artistry of Steel.'

Undoubtedly another telling factor was the outcome of the duel between arch-foes Steel and Aberdeen's Chris Anderson.

The press had speculated endlessly about how this would turn out and Steel added to the sense of anticipation by telling reporters: 'I'll beat him ten different ways, then I'll think of another ten ways.'

Dundee were now in the semi-final and on 29 March had to visit Easter Road, Edinburgh for the clash with Third Lanark.

It was a bitterly cold day and snow and sleet flurries had the crowd stamping their feet in an effort to keep warm. There was the inevitable comparison between Steel and his fellow Scotland inside forward Jimmy Mason, a player of sumptuous skills too often compromised by a lack of physical presence. On this day, Steel's star shone by far the brighter, despite his left ankle being heavily strapped. Initiating most of the Dark Blues' attacks, Billy created the first goal in 27 minutes when he rolled an inviting pass in front of Burrell who scored from eight yards.

Three minutes from half-time, Flavell found Steel just inside the Third Lanark half. Billy raced through the defence to score with an unsaveable shot from 15 yards.

The *Edinburgh Evening Dispatch* headline that day summed it up neatly: 'Two Steel flashes – Thirds pass out.'

The Scotsman's reporter at the game was so impressed by Steel's goal that he resorted to paraphrasing Oliver Goldsmith, the Irish poet and dramatist: 'I gazed and gazed and still the wonder grew, that one small man could hit so hard and true.' Dundee were in the final!

Due to injury, Billy was left out of the Scotland side which went down 2-1 to England at Hampden on 5 April.

'England,' wrote *The Times* of 7 April, 'Masters in teamwork and artistry left the Scots, lacking the inspiration of Steel, floundering and lucky to escape a heavier sentence.'

From international disappointment to national disaster, with the Scottish Cup final against Motherwell at Hampden on 19 April ending in a 4-0 defeat for Dundee. A record crowd for two provincial clubs – 136,274 – did not include the occupants of a railway 'special' from Dundee which arrived late. 1,000 furious fans were locked out.

The scoreline certainly flattered Motherwell but their method of harrassing Steel paid off. Billy was marked so tightly he could scarcely breathe.

Perhaps stung by criticism of their performance, Dundee rolled up their sleeves for the last league match of the season against Third Lanark at Dens on 26 April. Steel failed to score in the home side's 6-0 victory but was still the pick of the 22 players on the park, prompting and providing throughout the 90 minutes.

When the new season got under way on 9 August, Dundee beat Raith Rovers 2-1 at Dens in a League Cup encounter. The match had obviously given the Fifers something to think about. Before the return fixture at Stark's Park, Kirkcaldy on 23 August, the team and the coaching staff spent an entire forenoon on what was described as 'Operation Billy Steel'.

Whatever tactic they decided to adopt to try to shackle the Dundee star, it failed to work. Steel scored twice in the second half in the visitors' victory, again by 2-1.

Next Saturday, in Glasgow in the same competition, the Dark Blues took part in a nail-biting 3-3 draw with Clyde. 2-0 down at half-time, Dundee looked to their Scotland star for guidance. It was not long in coming. In the space of 10 minutes Steel transformed the game. In the 56th minute he delivered a shrewd pass to Christie, giving his wing partner a clear glimpse of goal … 2-1. Two minutes later, Billy produced one his trademark bursts into the penalty area, where he was unceremoniously floored. Alf Boyd scored from the penalty. 2-2. With 64 minutes on the clock, Steel found Flavell in a good position. The centre smacked the ball against the base of the post and Jimmy Toner put in the rebound. 3-2. Clyde, cruising along just minutes before now had to pull out all the stops to gain a share of the spoils.

In his column of 20 September in *The Sporting Post*, Rambler got in a dig at the selectors of the Scottish League teams, which had taken on an experimental look of late. Why had Steel been ignored? Rambler went on: 'He should be an automatic choice. He is playing as well as ever.' The columnist quoted one un-named selector who certainly agreed. 'I have seen several games in England where potential internationalists were playing. I have also seen most of our leading Scottish clubs. There just isn't an inside forward to compare with Steel.'

To ram home the point, Rambler spoke to a player who had recently opposed Steel. 'Billy,' said the defender, 'is the most devastating player in football today. I put this down to his amazing bursts of speed. From scratch he's off like a bullet and round you before you know what has happened.'

At the semi-final stage of the League Cup, Dundee were still there. The holders of the trophy faced a mountainous task in the all-ticket match against Hibs at Tynecastle on 4 October, especially as this was virtually a home game for the Edinburgh club, reigning league champions and whose forwards had notched up 40 goals between them in the course of a still-young season. Just a week before they had trounced the much-fancied Motherwell 7-3, away from home!

Beginning the second half 1-0 down, Reilly having scored, Dundee came more into the match and it was Steel who pulled them level in the 52nd minute with a tap-in from six yards. The match was now being played in a downpour.

A change of tactics saw Dundee now keeping almost every ball 'on the carpet' and with Steel in breathtaking form, they were proving much more incisive in their distribution than Hibs. They scored the winner through Flavell. The other semi had thrown up a real surprise, Kilmarnock from the B Division having defeated the mighty Rangers by a goal to nil.

The final was a dour affair, Dundee easing to a win by 2-0, although the top division side had been pushed all the way. The expected scenario of the Dundee attack versus the Killie defence was stood on its head and exactly the opposite occurred. Steel had a quiet game but it scarcely mattered. The Dens Parkers had won two trophies in the space of a year and reached the final of another.

When the Scottish League beat the Irish League 5-1 at Celtic Park on 8 October, Billy got on the score-sheet in the 34th minute when he met first-time a cross from Gordon Smith at the edge of the penalty area, driving in a fierce shot which flew high into the net. Lawrie Reilly scored a hat-trick. Billy's partner on the wing that day was another Hib, Willie Ormond, who was to become Scotland's manager in later years.

Billy actually 'spoiled' the one chance the Famous Five had of representing their country en bloc. Steel was the only non-Hib in the forward line-up, the unlucky player being Eddie Turnbull, who was a travelling reserve.

More international duty this time against Wales in Cardiff on 19 October saw Scotland win a tough encounter 2-1. The match afforded spectators the rare treat of being able to compare Steel, who despite many a darting dribble had not been his usual influential self, with the Welsh inside forward wizard, Ivor Allchurch, who tormented the Scottish defence for much of the 90 minutes.

The winning goal, scored in the 70th minute, was an astonishing effort. Steel swung a deep cross right over the Welsh defence. It was met by Liddell, whose diving header from 15 yards flew into the top of the net.

Now however, there were increasing worries about Steel, who had not been his usual bubbling self in recent weeks. He was dropped from the full national side for the first time in his life for the match against Ireland on 5 November.

He seemed to be struggling to compete. In the match against East Fife on 1 November, Dundee lost 3-2 despite that rare occurrence, a headed goal by Billy Steel whose contribution nevertheless fell well short of his accustomed standard.

The problem was finally identified – as a dental one! On the day he had eleven teeth extracted, Billy learned he had been reinstated in the Scotland side on the withdrawal of Alan Brown. Whether or not the visit to the dentist's chair had anything to do with it, Steel had an ineffective game for his country in a 1-1 draw which saw Reilly score a last-gasp equaliser.

Billy came in for some savage comments in the press. *The Evening Telegraph*'s issue of 6 November told him in no uncertain terms to get fit. 'At 29 he is not too old,' wrote the paper. 'Scotland can ill afford to lose his genius but for the moment he has lost the pace of international football.'

Scottish Schoolboys XI, with Billy (centre) in short trousers.

Steel and a good friend, George Young, relax on the golf course.

Left: Billy as a young player in the strip of Greenock Morton.

Below: The Scottish team which beat France 2-0 at Hampden Park in 1948. From left to right, back row: Alex Dowdells (Celtic, trainer), Waddell (Rangers), Cox (Rangers), Evans (Celtic), Cowan (Morton), Woodburn (Rangers), Aitken (East Fife), Telfer (St Mirren, reserve). Front row: Thornton (Rangers), Reilly (Hibs), Young (Rangers, captain), Steel (Derby County), Houliston (Queen of the South). Due to the fact that the French played in blue, as did Scotland, the home side turned out in an unusual primrose and pink strip.

Happy fans at Hampden before the 1948
match against England.

Billy Steel, a keen golfer, seen here receiving
a lesson at St Andrews shortly after joining
Dundee FC in 1950. Photograph courtesy
of St Andrews University Library.

Above: The Scotland party on their tour of America and Canada in the summer of 1949. From left to right, back row: Bobby Evans (Celtic), Willie Gall (newspaper reporter), Lawrie Reilly (Hibs), Billy Steel (Derby County). Middle row: Jack Govan (Hibs), Willie Thornton (Rangers), Alex Dowdells (Celtic, trainer), Alan Breck (newspaper reporter), Willie Telfer (St Mirren), George Young (Rangers). Front row: Willie Waddell (Rangers), Jimmy Brown (Hearts, goalkeeper), Tommy Orr (Morton), Willie Woodburn (Rangers), George Aitken (East Fife), Sammy Cox (Rangers), Willie Redpath (Motherwell), Johnny McKenzie (Partick Thistle). The photograph was taken on 4 June at Platzl's Brauhaus, Ladentown, New York.

Left: Despite his small stature, Steel was a fine header of the ball.

Above: The Scotland team which defeated Wales at Cardiff in 1950 by 3-1. From left to right, back row: Woodburn (Rangers), McColl (Rangers), Cowan (Morton), McPhail (Clyde), Forbes (Arsenal), McNaught (Raith Rovers). Front row: Collins (Celtic), Reilly (Hibs), Young (Rangers, captain), Steel (Dundee), Liddell (Liverpool).

Right: Steel in acrobatic pose. His training sessions included acrobatic moves and hand springs.

Alf Boyd leads out Dundee for their 1951 League Cup final clash with the mighty Glasgow Rangers.

George Young is the disconsolate Ranger after Pattillo put Dundee in front during the 1951 League Cup final at Hampden Park.

Left: The programme from the Scottish League Cup final. Dundee played Rangers in the match at Hampden Park on 27 October 1951.

Below: The League Cup on display at Dens after the victory over Rangers. From left to right, back row: Tommy Gallacher, Gerry Follon, Bill Brown, Doug Cowie, Jack Cowan. Middle row: Johnny Pattillo, Frank Graham (director), Bob Crichton (secretary), Andrew Clark (director), Jack Swadel (director), Reggie Smith (trainer). Front row: Jimmy Toner, Bobby Flavell, James Gellatly (chairman), Alf Boyd (captain), George Anderson (director/manager), Billy Steel, George Christie.

Dundee's League Cup-winning team of 1952, when they defeated Kilmarnock in the final.

Raith Rovers' John McLure launches into a tackle on Steel during a league match at Stark's Park, Kirkcaldy.

Above left: Billy Steel. *Above right:* A great Dundee favourite, George 'Pud' Hill.
Below left: Billy Steel. *Below right:* Director/manager George Anderson.

Above left: Wilf Mannion. *Above right:* Tom Finney.
Below left: Neil Franklin. *Below right:* Tommy Gallacher.

Goalkeeper Bill Brown watches anxiously as his defenders try to clear from a lone Rangers attack in the course of the match in February 1953 which set the all-time attendance record for Dens Park – 42,024.

Below left: Billy Steel in close contact with an Austrian defender during the infamous match in Vienna.
Below right: Billy trots forlornly off the field, the first Scot in modern times to be sent off in an international.

England 'keeper Matthews manages to get the ball away despite the close attentions of Lawrie Reilly.

Dundee's talented half-back line of Gallacher, Cowie and Boyd.

Reilly closes in on a cross from Hibs team-mate Gordon Smith as England's Dickinson and Hall move in to try to thwart the centre forward.

Bobby Evans.

Lawrie Reilly.

Above: Cigarette cards featuring Alf Ramsay and Billy Steel.

Below left: Bobby Brown, the Rangers goalkeeper, who also taught physical training at Denny High School. *Below right:* Jimmy Mason, of Third Lanark and Scotland, one of the most gifted inside rights ever to represent his country.

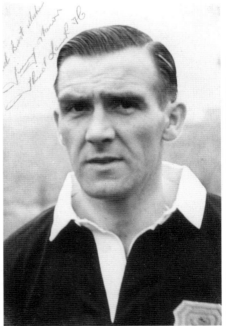

The party who combined so well to make Dundee's tour of South Africa and Rhodesia such a success. From left to right, back row: J. Stewart, A. Irvine, R. Henderson, G. Frew. Middle row: A. Henderson, J. Cowan, K. Ziesing, A. Boyd (captain), D. Cowie, R. Turnbull, R. Walker. Front row: G. Hill, F.H. Shackleton (South African Football Association), D. Easson, R. Crichton, R. Flavell, G. Adam, W. Steel, R. Smith (trainer), G. Christie.

Below left: Billy Steel keeps his eye on the ball during a training session at Dens Park. *Below right:* Sammy Cox of Rangers, a member of that club's famous 'Iron Curtain' defence and a seasoned international player.

A perfect picture of poise and balance as Billy Steel lets fly with one of his left-foot 'specials'.

Two Rangers and Scotland regulars. *Below left:* Outside right Willie Waddell, later to become manager of Rangers. *Below right:* Right-back George Young, captain of both club and country.

Billy was advised to get someone else to look after his Glasgow business and to concentrate on football, with more and more players now going full-time.

There is little doubt that Steel's approach to training was relaxed, to say the least. Billy's Dundee team-mate Tommy Gallacher made reference to his unorthodox methods:

'In those days our fitness schedule consisted of lapping the track, running up and down the terracing and the occasional road run. After a while, Billy would drift away from the other players. He would then perform an incredible selection of handsprings and acrobatics before practising with a ball. He trained when he wanted and he played when he felt like it. He was a law unto himself, but it was great to have him in your side on a Saturday. The fans thought he was a god.'

In his defence, it might be said he genuinely felt he needed less fitness work than other players. He had a great 'engine' and as his international colleague Willie Woodburn of Rangers noted: 'Billy could run for weeks.'

Billy shone in the next match at home to Airdrie. A 2-0 loss could not detract from the 'sparkle of Steel' though he was watched by two players for the entire match, a fact of life for Billy and never really taken into consideration when he had an off day.

Billy had plainly recovered from any health hangover he may have had when on 6 December he gave a memorable performance in a league match against Partick Thistle.

He scored a hat-trick in Dundee's 6-0 win. Dundee played 'draughtboard football' that day but the boot was on the other foot a week later when Billy was marked right out of the game against Celtic at Parkhead. The Glasgow side won 5-0.

Motherwell added to Dundee's woes the following Saturday when they won 2-1 despite Steel showing majestic form, working tirelessly to prise open the claret and amber defence. His pass in the last minute typified the game he had had. The ball was almost massaged into the path of Burrell who shot tamely past.

Billy was given the opportunity to captain Dundee in the festive season match against Queen of the South on 27 December. The game finished in a 0–0 draw but the best opportunity to score was created by Steel who clipped the ball to new boy Ian Stables, only for the youngster to mis-kick completely with the goal at his mercy.

-6-
Troubled Times

My outlook on this exceptional player is basically the view of a fan. But what of those whose task on the field of play was to confront Billy Steel and to try to cope with his unique skills?

International stars like George Young and Billy Wright for example. Young faced Steel four or five times a season on average and was full of admiration for what he was able to do. 'Almost impossible to dispossess,' wrote Young. 'Billy had this way of hanging over the ball...'

The Scotland captain knew Steel better than almost anyone. 'I first played against him when he was just thirteen and even then, admired his terrific ball control. Apart from his dainty feet and his quick-thinking brain, Billy Steel also possesses extraordinary strength for so small a laddie. Steel never goes half-heartedly into a tackle but always puts every ounce of his weight behind it and opponents all over Britain will confirm that the Dundee inside left tackles as well as any half-back.

'Steel is tremendously quick off the mark and the amazing stamina he has revealed enables him to put in a good deal of work in defence. To me, as a colleague and as an opponent, Steel's ability to start a move and then be up in the goal area to finish it, has never ceased to be a source of wonderment.'

Wright had faced Steel many a time when the Scot played for Derby, although not in direct opposition, Wright's usual club position being left half. For good measure, he played immediately opposite him in the Scotland-England matches.

'It was an education,' said Wright. 'You could be sure you would discover new and novel ways of being beaten.'

Lawrie Reilly rated him the most confident player he ever met.

'After the war he was the first superstar to go south and to make his mark. He had enormous faith in his own ability. Often, he would tell you what he was going to do, then he'd go and do it! I will never forget how, in the match against England in 1949 he and Willie Waddell just ran riot in the second half. He had the strongest legs I have ever seen on a footballer and although he was only five foot six or thereby, his upper body strength was exceptional too.'

Referring to the 1949 tour of the States and Canada, Reilly said: 'A few of the fellows were sitting round the resort swimming pool. For a laugh, Willie Woodburn and Geordie Young, probably our two biggest players, started shoving people into the water. Billy waited for Woodburn to come close then jumped up, lifted him off the ground and threw him bodily into the pool. Not bad considering Willie was over six feet!'

Steel's confidence – even arrogance – bore marked similarities to that shown by a later Scotland star, Jim Baxter. However, there the likeness comes to an end. Baxter was not in Steel's class. A wing half, his defensive capabilities hovered around zero. He could not tackle. Much of the reason for his inclusion at a very high level among the Scotland 'greats' centres upon the 1967 Wembley victory by 3-2 over the World Champions, England. There, he was much admired by many for taking the mickey out of England by playing 'keepy-up' – but not by me.

Baxter not only lost Scotland the one opportunity I can think of to visit upon the World Champions a resounding defeat, perhaps by

5-1 or 6-1, but he almost blew the match itself. It was a shame because until Slim Jim pressed the self destruct button he had been in inspired form. Once the nonsense took over, the Scots lost their shape. Their potent mix of power and class descended into a playground kick-about by juveniles and the Scots disappeared like leaves on a winter wind. To be fair, by no means did all the players abandon their professional standards. Just one team scored from that point on and that team was England.

For Dundee's first match of 1953, at Pittodrie against Aberdeen on 2 January, Billy captained the side in what turned out to be a ferocious encounter. Five Dundee players were injured, including Steel, who had to have an x-ray on a bruised leg.

Out through injury until 17 January, he pulled on the familiar number 10 jersey again for the home match against Raith Rovers. Raith were 2-0 up at half-time and seemingly heading for a comfortable win. In the 53rd minute, Steel changed all that when he accepted a pass from Gallacher on the halfway line, made as if to pass, then tore in on goal to strike a blistering drive past 'keeper Johnstone from 25 yards. It was a typically big goal from the smallest man on the park. Raith held on to win 3-2.

An unusual 'friendly' in the middle of the season saw Dundee entertain Hamilton Accies at Dens on 24 January. Steel seemed to revel in the relaxed atmosphere. In the 22nd minute he weaved his way past several defenders to the left touchline, looked up and directed centre forward Albert Henderson where to place himself. Steel's precision cross found Henderson's head and Dundee were one up.

The *Sporting Post* wrote that Steel, 'tired of laying on chances for others who won't take them' took a hand himself and in the space of as many minutes, produced three thunderbolts which brought out brilliant saves from 'keeper Ritchie.

Steel would not be denied. In the 53rd minute, surrounded by red and white jerseys, Billy still got in a scoring shot. Dundee ran out easy winners.

A draw against Hearts in Edinburgh on 2 February was characterised once again by some ugly fouls on Steel who, in total frustration, had a verbal exchange with the referee about it and got booked for his trouble.

Before the visit of Rangers in the second round of the Scottish Cup on 7 February, manager Anderson took a large party, including Steel, to indulge in a break, spiced with some special training, at Pitlochry. It didn't do much good. Rangers set Dundee a task they could not handle. The Ibrox outfit were in great nick, having gone 15 games without defeat. Their 'Iron Curtain' defence had conceded only seven goals in that spell. A new record crowd of 43,024, of which I was one, saw the visitors ease their way to a 2-0 win. My own memories of that match include the blunder by Dundee 'keeper Bill Brown who, with nobody near him, let a speculative cross slip through his fingers, run down his back and roll with comical slowness into the net. What I had really been looking forward to though, was a resumption of the rivalry between Steel and the Rangers right half, Ian McColl, whose full name was John Miller McColl.

These great players, both internationalists, had for some time provided the Scottish footballing public with one of the great head-to-head duels of the early 1950s. On this occasion, the cultured McColl, tackling with the speed and accuracy of a striking cobra, came out well on top. When the final whistle blew I can recall vividly being 'transported' out of Dens Park by the crowd for the last 100 or so yards, my feet quite failing to make any contact with the ground, such was the press of people. The thought of what could have happened if someone in front had fallen still sends a shiver down my spine.

A week later, on Valentine's Day, Rangers went to Dens again, this time on league business. Dundee competed far more effectively here and earned a 1-1 draw.

The hunt for league points continued with the visit of East Fife on 21 February, this match also ending 1-1. Steel virtually ran the show. Jockeying for position in the penalty box he was floored by the attentions of no fewer than three Fifers. No penalty!

The second half saw Steel in even more dominant mood as he fought to overcome a single goal deficit. In one incident he 'turned several circles in the goalmouth, beating a host of opponents, some of them two or three times' but could find no room to get in a shot. In the 56th minute Dundee were back on level terms. In 'a Steel-inspired move', Burrell netted the equaliser.

The amount of punishment being dished out to Steel was causing growing unease and George Anderson announced on Wednesday 4 March that for the visit of Hibs on the Saturday, Steel would be at outside left 'owing to the recent treatment he has received on the field'. This was an oblique swipe at referees, seen to be doing too little to protect such players and it was certainly true that sendings off for bad fouls were rare happenings in those days. But then, as now, the officials found themselves in the bad books of managers whose comments continue in the same self-centred vein. In early days referees put up with all the insults for five guineas per match plus third-class rail tickets to get them to and from the ground. Linesmen got £2 10s each.

This league match, played out before a crowd of 30,000, saw Steel cross from his unaccustomed position for Flavell to score, and he then cut in from the wing in the 70th minute to score himself in Dundee's 2-0 victory.

Still on the wing for the visit of Falkirk on 14 March, Steel delighted the crowd with 'some fancy football on the left'. However it seemed obvious as the match progressed that Billy had been given a roving commission. On the right touchline he took the ball past three defenders before swinging over an inviting cross for Flavell, whose shot was blocked. The game ended in a 2-1 win for Dundee, Steel having scored the winner in the 70th minute 'arriving at full throttle' to bang the ball home.

On Saturday 28 March, Steel was in his usual berth at inside left as Dundee ran out 3-0 winners in the league match at Firhill against Partick Thistle, Steel having notched the second. Manager Anderson decided to play Steel, even though he had a broken toe!

For Dundee's final home game of the season they played host to Celtic on 4 April. Steel celebrated the occasion with a superb display. He created the first goal for Flavell, beating three men before teeing it up. Although he failed to score in Dundee's 4–0 victory, Billy produced perhaps the biggest roar of the afternoon when he almost shattered the crossbar with an 83rd-minute drive.

His form boded well for the international against England at Wembley on 18 April and when that game duly arrived, watched among other celebrities by the entire Australian cricket team, Billy was singled out for comment in the half-time summary of the *Sporting Post*: 'Steel has grafted away but all his prompting of team-mates has broken down on the 18-yard line.' Billy almost scored himself, hitting the bar just before the interval. 2–1 down, Scotland's cause seemed to be lost when, with 20 minutes to go, left-back Cox had to be stretchered from the field. Dundee's Doug Cowie was moved from left half to left-back while Steel took over Cowie's berth. The ten-man Scots continued to threaten and shots from both Liddell and Steel hit the bar.

Again it was Reilly with seconds remaining, who scored a wonderful equaliser, ignoring the proximity of full-back Alf Ramsey to lob the ball coolly over the 'keeper's head, thus reaffirming his nickname of 'Last-minute Reilly', a label he always regarded as an invention of the press and consequently viewed it with some disdain.

As the final whistle blew, Reilly remembers that Sammy Cox came hobbling onto the pitch and, throwing away his crutches, gave him a huge hug. Steel's contribution was described as showing 'many brilliant flashes. He was unlucky not to have scored three goals'. Scotland had again secured the International Championship, without losing a match.

Billy had one more international to play before the turnstiles fell silent for the season, against Sweden at Hampden. The Swedes came away with a 2–1 victory but despite their clever passing game, they should never have gone home with the spoils. Steel, easily the best Scot on view, created three gilt-edged chances in the first half for the Hibernian inside right Bobby Johnstone but he could take none of them.

Football got under way again on 8 August with Dundee entertaining Stirling Albion in a League Cup A Division match. Dundee seemed to have benefited from a summer tour of South Africa where their record was: Played 17; Won 15; Lost 1; Drawn 1. They looked yards faster than their opponents. Steel scored twice in their 6-1 win. After a draw with Partick Thistle, Dundee beat Stirling Albion again, in Stirling on 22 August, by 2-0.

Dundee's next match, versus Clyde at Dens on Wednesday 26 August, ended in a 4-2 win for the home team. Steel's almost magical exhibition was exemplified by his goal in the 33rd minute when he controlled a pass from Christie, side-stepped centre half Campbell and chipped the advancing 'keeper.

After the match, Clyde's recently-appointed trainer Dawson Walker said: 'Billy's form was a sheer delight.' Manager Paddy Travers said of the Dundee star: 'He had the most to do with our defeat.' Travers somehow contrived to avoid making any mention of his defenders' brutal treatment of the same man throughout the match.

The home fixture against Raith on 12 September in the league was summed up by the *Sporting Post* as 'a most amazing game'. The scoreline read 0-0, but the visitors were never in it. Dundee's forwards, dogged by bad luck all day, saw several shots rebounding from the woodwork, one of these being a rocket from Steel.

Acting captain Steel led his team to a 2-0 victory over Clyde at Dens on 26 September, scoring himself in the 32nd minute.

The captain's armband now decorating the left limb of Doug Cowie, Dundee romped to a 4-1 win over Queen of the South at Dens on 10 October, Steel having got on the score-sheet courtesy of a gloriously-struck daisy-cutter in the 59th minute. A watching selector, Jimmy Beattie, could hardly fail to have been impressed by Steel's performance.

This was a significant victory for the Dens Parkers. Not only were Queens top of the table, but they had been in danger of becoming something of a bogey side to them. On their previous two visits to Dens they had been totally outplayed but still came away with a point each time.

It was also the match that launched Dundee into a phase of prime form during which they took three points out of a possible four in matches against the Old Firm. They beat Rangers 1-0 on 24 October, Steel making the most of a match when he was said to be 'on trial' and in direct comparison with Rangers' John Prentice who was challenging him for the Scotland inside left berth.

'Here, there and everywhere', Steel gave the Ibrox defenders a torrid time. The Celtic game ended 1-1 a week later. In an odd incident in the latter game, Steel may have scored the equaliser. His header against the underside of the bar in the 65th minute was thought to have crossed the line, but the rebound was put in by Cowie just to make sure. Neither player was credited with the goal!

Billy's burst of supreme form did him no good in the eyes of the selectors. For the match against Wales in early November his place went to, not Prentice, but Blackpool's Alan Brown. Steel's last game for Dundee for quite a spell came at Broomfield on 14 November. He scored in the 2-2 draw with Airdrie. And what an odd counter it was. Trying one of his 'specials' from outside the box, he made a poor contact with the ball, which trundled sedately towards goalkeeper Fraser. Poor Fraser completely failed to make any contact with the shot which had just enough pace left to get over the line.

On Monday 14 November, Dundee had a friendly floodlight date with Leeds United at Elland Road. It could have provided quite a talking point for Leeds were managed by Raich Carter, who played for part of the match. Steel, however, was not in the Dundee team which lost 2-0.

Billy found himself 'rested' for the match against Stirling Albion the following week but was not selected for the next three games either, the furious speculation arising from this being dismissed by George Anderson with a curt 'no comment'. However, the truth was that Billy had again managed to upset his team-mates and this time Anderson sided with the majority, who were becoming increasingly disenchanted with this supremely gifted but domineering colleague.

Tommy Gallacher said: 'Steel was one of football's greatest characters and he could beat a man any number of ways. However, he could be a bit of a tyrant on the field and if you didn't do things the way he felt they should be done you would hear about it. Wherever he went, the fur was sure to fly. Having said that, the more his tongue wagged, the better he seemed to play!'

Even in those magical 'high' moments after the scoring of a goal, Steel could still find the time to have a go. On his way back to the centre circle after scoring, Pattillo was told sarcastically: 'It took you a wee while to think about that one Johnny!'

Gallacher himself was almost driven to distraction on one occasion and entered the dressing room at half-time, vowing violence against his team-mate. Luckily, goalkeeper Johnny Lynch managed to calm him down.

It proved difficult for frustrated colleagues to find ways to hit back when Steel could put on the most magical displays even under circumstances which might be described as 'not ideal.' Gallacher provided a classic example, referring to one New Year's Day clash at Dens with Aberdeen, a match dominated by a 'very relaxed' Steel.

'It being that time of year,' said Tommy, 'Billy had been out all night and he really hadn't much idea where he was. He was staying in the RB Hotel, Dundee and I picked him up in Reform Street to take him to the game. He was the worse for wear so I took him to his room and tidied him up a bit. Honestly, he was half gassed but he tore Aberdeen apart that day. I think George Anderson knew what was going on but he turned a blind eye.'

Billy was back on duty for the league match at Kirkcaldy against Raith on Boxing Day. As he ran onto the park he got a resounding cheer all to himself.

Dundee won 2-1 with Billy producing his best form. Dundee's equaliser was described as a Steel product. He picked up the ball in midfield and beat three men before passing to Henderson who moved it on for Toner to score.

As Dundee began 1954 with a Ne'er Day victory over Clyde at Dens, no one at the club or on the terraces could have guessed that this was destined to be the year when Billy Steel's football career ground to an untimely halt. There was no hint of any of this when Steel took centre stage for the 3-2 defeat of Hamilton Accies in a league fixture in Dundee on 9 January. Billy scored in 33 minutes and, with a piece of sorcery only he could have conjured up, left two men floundering in his wake before cutting the ball back from the bye-line for right-winger Carmichael to score the third goal.

The visit of league leaders Hearts on 23 January again had Steel in inspirational mood as Dundee took the field in a white strip. In one awesome moment he delivered a full-blooded cross from the left by means of a soaring back heel which almost allowed Toner to score. Dundee were nevertheless up against it and Hearts were two up before Dundee could get on the score-sheet through Doug Cowie.

The half-time summary described Steel's equalising strike in the 44th minute as 'a goal in a million'. In a series of bewildering feints he beat two defenders before hammering the ball into the net from 15 yards.

The *Sporting Post*'s reporter at the game went on: 'Steel's goal will be a topic of conversation for many a day.' Billy trotted out for the second half and proceeded to give a demonstration of soccer artistry which ought to have seen his side home and dry. Two goals from Conn in the final ten minutes however, gave Hearts the points. It was the first time they had beaten Dundee in a league match at Dens since the war.

February was a highly forgettable month for Dundee. They lost to Rangers at Ibrox and to Celtic by 5-1, also in Glasgow. Steel, out for part of the month with flu, was still the Dark Blues' top-scorer with seven goals for the season thus far. That spoke volumes for Dundee's difficulties in front of goal for the division's top-scorer was Charlie 'Cannonball' Fleming of East Fife with no fewer than 32 goals.

Lowest point of the month came at Second Division Berwick in the third round of the Scottish Cup on 27 February. Even with Steel back in the line-up, Dundee seemed bereft of ideas and the jubilant lower leaguers ran out easy winners by 3 goals to nil.

Dundee bounced back to win 3-2 in a tough league encounter away to Stirling Albion on 13 March but suffered a 2-0 defeat at Easter Road. Steel, never one to hide his opinions on the park, probably had something to say about the 'sitters' he set up for Henderson in the first half and for George Merchant in the second.

Steel, in the middle of an inconsistent spell, failed to enter the minds of the selectors when on 23 March they chose the Scotland team to play England at Hampden on 3 April. He had been watched by selector Harry Swan during Dundee's losing visit to Easter Road on 20 March and Swan had said after the game: 'I can't recommend Billy Steel for the Scottish team on that form.'

This loss of form was perhaps predictable, for Billy was now playing with an injured ankle numbed by an injection before every game. He had refused an operation and it was feared his career might end prematurely. But he showed he was still able to deliver the goods for his team and in the league encounter with East Fife at Bayview on the same day that Scotland were going down to England, he was, according to the *Sporting Post*, 'producing the only spark in the Dundee attack'.

In the 57th minute, Billy brought about the equaliser after leaving three defenders wondering where he'd gone. His shot could only be parried by 'keeper Curran into the path of Merchant, who scored. The final score was 1-1.

Dundee's last league match of the season at Dens saw them defeat Partick Thistle by 6-0. Steel, who did not score, had the ball in the net twice, with both 'goals' being chalked off for offside.

Rambler's Roundup in the *Sporting Post* of 1 May spoke of rumours 'flying round Glasgow' that Rangers were about to sign Steel.

The rumours, it turned out, were the result of a rift which had arisen between Billy and George Anderson. When Steel signed for Dundee, part of the deal was that he would be permitted to train in Glasgow, at Clyde's ground, Shawfield, and also have a job – in this case running his shop, which was not uncommon for professional footballers of the period.

Although Steel had given up his shop, Anderson was now beginning to suspect that Billy was not training regularly and issued an ultimatum – train full-time at Dens on three or four days every week or face possible transfer. Steel refused to comply despite being offered 'top terms' for the following season and Anderson went public with the comment: 'We'll now listen to offers from other clubs.'

Billy was not selected for the match against Aberdeen on Monday 19 April. Off his own bat, Steel travelled to Aberdeen anyway and, on the withdrawal of George Merchant, offered to play anywhere in the forward line. He played in the match, at inside left.

But a sea change was under way at Dundee Football Club. Mr Anderson was about to hand over the managerial reins to the former Rangers centre forward Willie Thornton and as Thornton came in, Billy Steel was already on his way out, having taken the decision to bring down the curtain on his own playing days at the age of thirty-one.

He had made 131 appearances for Dundee and scored 45 goals. The news was carried in *The Courier & Advertiser* of 5 July when Steel said he had written to Dundee FC indicating he was giving up football. The club denied they had ever received such a letter and it is probably accurate to say that in Billy they had found a difficult customer to deal with. Steel went on to say he was about to take an extended holiday in America with his wife Lillian and their two children, Billy (aged five) and Hilary (aged three). When he returned to Scotland, he would never play senior football again.

-7-
California

It was *The People's Journal*, later in the month, which broke the real story. Billy had landed a job as manager of one of the top sides in California, the Los Angeles Danes.

Although this was unpaid, the entire soccer set-up in the area being strictly amateur, Billy had also secured a position as an advertising agent with a Los Angeles newspaper. Included in the arrangement was a house and a car, according to the paper's Gordon Gray in its issue of 31 July.

'Billy can earn about 600 dollars a month, four times what he could have earned in Scotland as a player,' wrote Gray.

It was revealed that the man behind Billy's move was Glasgow-born businessman Alistair Brannan, now a Californian, who also made certain that the local Scots exiles would lay on for the Steel family a welcome they would never forget.

It was a black day for Scottish football, however, when on Thursday 12 August, Billy and his wife and two children, all suitably innoculated to comply with US immigration laws, boarded the *Queen Elizabeth* at Southampton and sailed for the United States. It was a black day for Dundee FC in particular, minus any fee for losing Steel and about to enter upon a period of decline in which their departing star was desperately missed.

The financial rewards for playing football, already referred to, were a contentious issue among players and in Billy's book the 'summing up' section dealt with the wages aspect of that era (the book was published in 1948).

Billy wrote: 'The successful player, as represented by the Players' Union, can expect a maximum of £12 per week in the playing season, £10 a week in the close season. Bonuses are: £2 for a win, £1 for a draw.' (These were all maximum figures.) Extra bonuses were allowed by the FA for teams winning League and Cup competitions. A player was entitled to a benefit after five years' service with a club, the actual amount to depend on how many times he appeared for the first team. The most he could receive was £750. If a player was transferred after, say, three years, the accrued benefit would be worth about £450.

It was all very paltry for players who kept millions of fans entertained with their skills and the shame of the matter lay in the fact that there was no good financial reason for this level of tight-fistedness on the part of the FA and the SFA.

In contrast with the general state of the UK economy, there was plenty of money in football. The clubs were doing well out of the massive attendances they were getting and although entry fees to the grounds were low, so were club expenses on items like travel and the purchase of equipment. Clubs spent little or no money on their stadiums and some of them were positively dangerous as a result. Facilities for fans were simply not considered and the medieval cess-pits that passed for toilets bore ripe witness to this disgusting state of affairs.

Billy, who had never been slow to voice his disapproval of the wages structure, gave by way of example the case of Tommy Lawton as being about the best any player could squeeze out of the game. He acknowledged that the England centre forward was a shrewd businessman who had several fingers in several pies.

'On his transfer from Chelsea to Notts County it was reported that £20,000 changed hands. Tom had also secured a long-term contract with an industrial concern which, together with royalties from his football books and his newspaper column, has put him in the £3,000 a year class.'

Billy had his own ways of turning the odd penny. One deal in which he was involved concerned Cholertons shoe warehouse in Green Lane, Derby. At Cholertons, the late Frank Roome was given the task of designing the Billy Steel football boot for which the shop had the franchise. Mr Roome and Billy travelled to London to have the player's signature registered for transfer to the boots. Billy's end of the deal? Sixpence for each pair sold. In his book, Billy proffered advice in the business of buying boots. 'I take a size six to six and a half in shoes but only four and a half or five in football boots. They'll stretch all right and as they stretch they will conform to the shape of your feet. Buy boots the same size as your shoes and they'll be too big in no time.'

Billy also wrote a column for the *News Chronicle* while with Derby which may have provided the money to allow him to run a car – not a common thing for a footballer and something which got right under the skin of his colleagues at the Midlands club.

The Californian league in which Billy's team played consisted of sixteen teams, each with its own ethnic identity. Apart from a Scots side in San Francisco, there were teams consisting entirely of Poles, Germans and Mexicans, among others, rendering every match an international! Among supporters of the Los Angeles Danes were Hollywood legends Bing Crosby, James Stewart, Donald O'Connor and Spencer Tracy. Billy enjoyed meeting these celebrities and he handled with aplomb situations which others might have found intimidating.

Billy's contractural obligations to Dundee initially prohibited him from turning out for his team, which played on Sundays between May and September on 'proper' soccer grounds, not in converted baseball stadia. The games were well attended and often regarded as ideal for family outings. Fathers would pay 75 cents to get into the ground, mothers half that and children got in for free. Lunches, teas and other refreshments were available.

Billy's association with Dundee Football Club came to a somewhat bizarre end during January 1956 when he was transferred to the Los Angeles Danes for a nominal fee of £1,000. Billy presumably passed on to his new players some of the training tips he himself set down in his book, such as the avoidance of swimming, which was held to be bad for footballers. He may also have tried to enforce another restriction which applied to British players. Clubs frowned on ballroom dancing, which was an extremely popular pastime in the 1950s. With most matches played on Saturdays, dancing was forbidden on any day after Wednesday.

However, in car-conscious California he might have had some trouble in persuading his players to adopt another piece of perceived wisdom from the United Kingdom. There, players were instructed never to drive to any football match. It was a reasonable rule as any motor accident involving a team member would leave the rest 'high and dry.'

Billy settled in Lancaster, a high desert town in the Antelope Valley north of Los Angeles. And it was in Lancaster during 1971, firstly at the bar in a local motel, that Billy came into contact with football fans from Derby and they often talked over old times. The Derby group were part of a highly-skilled Rolls Royce outfit helping to support Lockheed, then building the TriStar aircraft at nearby Palmdale.

Billy never forgot his roots and regularly returned to Scotland to visit his mother, Mrs Elizabeth Sutherland and his sister, both of whom remained in Denny. He also went north to see his son Billy, who was now living and working in Aberdeen.

Tommy Gallacher had kept in contact with Billy, who despite his often exasperating behaviour was still regarded with affection by his former team-mates, whose nickname for him was Budgem.

One reason for this popularity was his off-the-field persona. Gallacher wrote of him: 'Off the park you couldn't meet a better bloke. We used to join him at D.M. Brown's in Dundee High Street on match days and by the time we got to Dens he'd have told us fifty jokes. It was a privilege to know him.'

Tommy met Billy every time he returned to his homeland. The last time Tommy saw him was on his final trip back in 1980.

'He was not a well man,' said Gallacher. 'He had always been a heavy smoker and he liked his dram. He was easily the best player ever to represent Dundee, but if only he had looked after himself, what might he have done?'

On Wednesday 12 May 1982, Billy was taken to hospital in Los Angeles where he died at 8 p.m. the following day.

Among the many tributes to this supreme footballer was one from former Morton manager Hal Stewart: 'We have lost one of the all-time greats.'

Stewart knew Billy well and in the early 1950s, on every other Friday during the season, he would pick him up outside his shop and drive him to Dundee for home games.

Stewart had close connections with Dundee FC and of the record fee the club paid for Steel, he said: 'It was just like Brian Clough paying £1 million for Trevor Francis in a later age. And Billy was well worth it. You could build a team round him. 'I will always remember during Dundee's tour to South Africa in 1953 how Billy just thrilled everyone out there. They had never seen anything like it.'

Willie Woodburn said: 'Everybody liked him. Except his opponents!'

Woodburn generally shared a room with Billy before international matches and recalled his diminutive team-mate sitting up in bed reading and chain-smoking into the small hours.

'Don't you think you'd better get some sleep, Billy?' asked Woodburn.

'What's the worry?' came the reply. 'It's only England tomorrow!'

Dundee and Scotland team-mate Doug Cowie said: 'He was some boy to get on with but I think that was because he was an out-and-out perfectionist. I liked him a lot. He was a great lad.'

Cowie's remark was a shrewd one. During one international match in the Portuguese capital, Lisbon, Celtic's Bobby Evans walked off the field and told the Scotland bench in no uncertain terms that something would have to be done about Steel's comments. At a subsequent meeting to clear the air, Steel was unrepentant.

He told his team-mates: 'Once a player thinks he's good enough, that's when he starts slipping. A player should be his own most severe critic. If I make a mistake, go ahead and shout at me. Criticise as much as you like. I won't object.'

The unfortunate Evans became the target for Steel in a different way, for it was not just with his fellow professionals that Steel could show his waspish side. He seemed to have had something of a love-hate relationship with Scotland's seven selectors. On one occasion they managed to make it known that Steel was on the verge of being dropped from the international side and they turned up en masse to see Celtic play Dundee at Parkhead. Among those in the know it was felt that Steel would have to produce something exceptional that day. Typically, he did.

Shortly after the kick-off, Steel acquired the ball and made a bee-line for Evans, his immediate opponent. He nut-megged the right half, turned round to face his own goal and nut-megged him again. He then danced through two tackles before laying on the ball for Flavell to tap into the net. On the way back to the centre circle Billy looked up at the selectors' box and grinned!

With Billy's death, a familiar and well-trodden football field fell silent for a minute when at Dens on Saturday 15 May as players and fans of Dundee and Airdrie paid their tribute to Steel and to former Dundee manager Bob Shankly who had also died in recent days.

Lifelong Dundee supporter Charles Wellwood, who now lives in Newmills, by Dunfermline, was as badly affected as anyone. He said: 'I have treasured memories of all the post-war Dundee greats. Alan Gilzean, Alfie Boyd, Charlie Cook, Alex Hamilton, Bobby Cox, Ian Ure and in more recent times, Claudio Caniggia.

'But in Billy Steel, Dundee had something almost beyond description. Even on his off days – and Billy had a few – you could always count on a moment or two of pure magic. These alone were worth the admission money.

'When he was in prime form he could dismantle a team like no one else I watched in 50 years of following the game. He was unique. A one-off.'

-8-
The Final Whistle

Steel was not just the best player to grace the city of Dundee. He may have been the most gifted individual ever to pull on a Scotland jersey. He scored 12 goals (not including tours) while earning his 31 caps, a total which disqualifies him from entry to the Scottish Football Hall of Fame for which 50 caps is the magic number. The fact that this permits a number of mere grafters to get in ahead of Steel seems to have no bearing on the matter at all. Included among Steel's caps were those he earned playing at Wembley in 1947, 1949, 1951 and 1953 where his record was: Won 2, Drawn 2. Steel took part in several overseas tours with Scotland. One cap was awarded for an entire tour, not one for each match played, so he actually represented his country more often than is generally believed.

In promoting the case for a particular player to be the best, we need to be clear about how we define 'the best'. The type of player who is capable of turning in fine, dependable performances for his country, game after game, cannot enter the equation, even though he may indeed be the most valuable kind of player to have on your team.

The benchmark is genius, and it is, hard to find. In its ultimate form it can make the hairs on the back of your neck can stand on end. This curious physical reaction, in its permanent silence, speaks with an eloquence far more profound than anything the tongue or the pen can deliver. In my case, only Billy Steel could produce this effect – a man I had never met did that for me, a player whose gifts I got to share at the astonishing rate of one shilling and sixpence a throw.

I am aware of course that 'the best' exists only as an insupportable concept in the mind of the fan. Especially as his thoughts may be the least rational of any human being. For him, the stonewall penalty at one end becomes the despicable dive at the other. His notion of 'the best' has no logical merit. His claim must always be impossible to substantiate. What of all those stars he had never even seen?

What of those worshipped by other fans, each with a dozen reasons why *their* favourite was 'the best'? None of us can make a case for the man of his choice that would stand up to close examination. But I'm going to have a crack at it, trying to look at Steel as dispassionately as I can manage under a number of headings.

SKILL LEVELS

No one could touch Billy that I ever saw. Not only was he capable of spasms of outrageous genius, but he could do it at pace. It was a combination I feel, looking back, that goes part of the way to explain why so many of the chances he created were not taken. Whether playing for Scotland or for Dundee, his footballing brain seemed a thought or two in advance of some of his team-mates. Time and again I watched him confuse defenders without touching the ball and he had that instinctive ability, as Liverpool fans used to say of Steve Heighway in the 1970s, that could even send the crowd the wrong way!

One of his favourite manoeuvres was to approach a defender, stop, and then kick the ball against the man's shins. The tactic always seemed to induce in the opponent a sense of bewilderment and while he was trying to reassemble his senses, Billy would have taken the rebound, put it left or right of the man or through his legs and then round him in a flash. Despite his small stature, he was a fine header of the ball. In his instruction book on the game, Billy told of once watching a conjuror on stage performing amazing feats with a ball and in trying to emulate the performer, he spent hour after hour heading the ball into the air, bouncing it lower and lower until it rested on his forehead. He once used this acquired skill during a match in Germany and ran about 15 yards with the ball balanced on his forehead.

STRENGTH AND FITNESS

There were whispers from time to time about Billy's fitness – and with some justification. Yet, when you'd seen him covering every blade of grass in his efforts to lift his team, you could marvel not only at the man's natural staying power, but at his ability to finish games more full of running than team-mates with less exacting roles. Billy's book devotes a whole chapter to the subject of training, going into great detail, but the reality was a lot different. In the 1940s especially, training was not as organised as Billy would have had his readers believe. With older players, trainers tended to leave them to their own devices and at Derby people like Raich Carter would often not train at all preferring as he put it, to 'save myself for Saturday'. So laid back was the general atmosphere that someone at Derby might ask: 'Who are we playing on Saturday?' Sometimes the fixture list would have to be consulted to discover the answer.

Billy did sometimes fade from games in the second half, but a reason for this other than lack of fitness should be considered. There was no question that he was often nursing an injury and since no substitutes were allowed in his day, injured players tended to soldier on somehow, usually confined to limping around on the wing, of little more than nuisance value.

On many an occasion I found myself wincing at some of the tackles he had to endure. *The Courier & Advertiser*'s Colin Glen, writing about the Dundee *v.* St Mirren match of 28 February 1953, mentioned that his notebook contained details of no fewer than seven fouls committed against Steel before half-time. I could have told Mr Glen that this was par for the course. Such routine brutality often failed for Billy's strength was legendary.

Probably treated more harshly than any other forward of his generation in Scotland, this hard little man learned to retain control of the ball better than anyone in the face of the most desperate efforts to dispossess him. Today's fans must also bear in mind that ball players were not as well protected in Billy's era as they are now. Sendings off were rare.

Tommy Gallacher recounted another tale which demonstrated that the man was as tough as his name.

'Billy's calf muscles were bigger than my thigh muscles and he was able to shrug off tackles by players almost twice his size. He was as strong as an ox. In one game at Dens he was tormenting the Celtic defence as only he could. The centre half, big John McGrory, decided to do something about it. He did, and got carried off on a stretcher for his pains!'

Another factor which elevated Steel from the pack of gifted ball-players of his time was his ability to tackle. Hugely impressive in his winning of the ball, he often left bigger, heavier opponents gasping and winded on the turf. Billy's own advice on preparing to tackle, as explained in his book, was: 'You must be balanced evenly on both feet. Never get up on your toes as an opponent comes near. Get the weight forward, crouch a little, tiger–like, and be ready to move in any direction. Remember that while an opponent can swerve or sway, the ball cannot. So never take your eye off the ball when going into a tackle.'

Strength played a part too in the type of goal for which Billy was renowned. He packed one of the hardest shots in football. Not known as a poacher hunting for tap-ins, Billy's range tended to be 15 yards plus. And if anyone scored more truly spectacular goals, I never saw that person play.

READING THE GAME

When no one else could see an opening Steel did and time after time he put into practice one of his own favourite phrases: 'Football is a game of wits.' The hackneyed saying 'a goal out of nothing' might have been invented with Billy in mind. It bespoke a speed of thought that, allied to the speed with which that thought was put into effect, produced gem after gem for the fan to savour, which can still be recalled by dint of its sheer perfection as though it were yesterday. Billy was sometimes criticised by his own team-mates for hounding them constantly in his appeals for the ball. Annoying it may have been, but who among them could say, with hand on heart, that any other member of the side could come close to matching *his* knack of unlocking the most resolute defence? It was obvious that Billy relished playing against Rangers. The reason, I believe, was that the great Ibrox defence offered him the greatest challenge in Scottish football. Certainly he appeared to take particular delight in unlocking it!

LEADERSHIP

Leadership might also be described as inspiration. Not in the sense of the job of a captain on the field but in terms of ability *he* was the player looked to deliver something special in times of adversity and there is little doubt that his own self-belief bred confidence in others. Considering the close watching he was always subjected to, it amazed me how often he was able to produce inspirational performances.

CHARISMA

In footballing terms this means for me the innate capacity to sear into the minds of those who saw him play, moments which you just knew could never be replicated by anyone else. Many other great players have shown themselves over and over again able to do great things, but to truly excite? That's something else again. For The Beautiful Game as Billy played it really was beautiful.

Rising above the 'professional' fouls, the jersey tugging, the attempts to con referees, the time wasting, the infantile theft of a yard or two at throw-ins and free-kicks and the endless expectorating, a precious few like Steel were still able to present the world's most popular game as living art.

The final word might best be left to an opponent. Jock Buchanan, who played against Steel many times for his club, Clyde, once complained: 'I hate playing against Dundee. I can't concentrate on my own game for watching Billy Steel!'

That then, is the case. Rip it to pieces if you will. All I know is that, although Billy Steel is no longer with us, he lives still, in the minds, in the hearts, in the recollections of those lucky enough to have stood shoulder to shoulder on terracings of freezing mud to watch him exhibit his matchless skill under the grey, winter skies of the land of his birth.

Bibliography

How To Play Football – Billy Steel – *Billy Wright's Book of Soccer, No. 1*
The Big Book of Football Champions
The FA Book for Boys (1951/52)
Stanley Matthews Football Album
Greenock Morton Football Club, 1874–1999
There Was Some Football Too (Derby County Centenary Book)
   – Tony Francis
Up Wi' The Bonnets (The Centenary History of Dundee Football Club)
   – Norrie Price
Captain of Scotland – George Young
Dundee Greats – Jim Hendrie
The Scottish Football Book – edited by Hugh Taylor
The Sporting Post – 29 April 1950; 29 September 1950;
   4 November 1950; 1 March 1952; 24 January 1953;
   18 April 1953; 12 September 1953; 23 January 1954;
   3 April 1954; 1 May 1954; 8 May 1954
The Courier & Advertiser – 28 April 1949; 11 December 1950;
   24 January 1951; 28 May 1951; 5 July 1954
The Times – 14 April 1947; 16 April 1951; 7 April 1952
The Scotsman – 10 November 1949; 2 November 1950;
   29 October 1951; 10 March 1952; 31 March 1952
The Evening Telegraph – 29 October 1951; 6 November 1952
The People's Journal – 17 October 1950; 31 July 1954; 7 August 1954
Edinburgh Evening Dispatch – 29 March 1952

Index

Index

Index